Key Stage 2 Maths

WORKBOOK 3

Numerical Reasoning Technique

Dr Stephen C Curran

with Katrina MacKay

Edited by Andrea Richardson

This book belongs to

ae
PUBLICATIONS

Accelerated Education Publications Ltd

Contents

Chapter Four
MULTIPLICATION
1. Multiplication Terms

Multiplication is the process of increasing the same number a given amount of times. It is a form of repeated addition.

For example:

If there are **4** bicycles, each with **2** wheels, altogether there are **8** wheels.

4 groups of **2** together becomes **8**.

This is often represented in a number sentence, such as:

$$4 \times 2 = 8$$

This symbol means 'multiply by'

The answer is called the 'product'

Multiplication can also be called 'scaling'. Here are two skyscrapers, one is twice as high as the other.

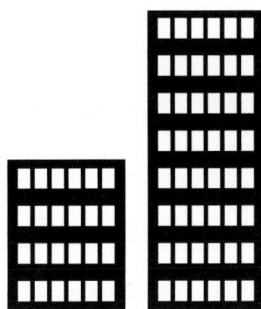

The first skyscraper has **4** floors and the second has **8** floors. This means the second building has been scaled up and is two times as high.

Multiply also means 'times', e.g. **4** times **2** equals **8**. Multiplication calculations give the same answer when written the other way round:

$$4 \times 2 = 8 \text{ is the same as } 2 \times 4 = 8$$

2. Multiplication by 0

When multiplying by **zero** the answer will always be **zero**.

For example, if there are **five** classes with **zero** children in each class, then the total number of children is **zero** or **none**.

$$5 \times 0 = 0$$

If there are **zero** or **no** children in the **five** classes, then the total number of children is **zero** or **none**.

$$0 \times 5 = 0$$

$0 \times 0 = 0$
$1 \times 0 = 0$
$2 \times 0 = 0$
$3 \times 0 = 0$
$4 \times 0 = 0$
$5 \times 0 = 0$
$6 \times 0 = 0$
$7 \times 0 = 0$
$8 \times 0 = 0$
$9 \times 0 = 0$
$10 \times 0 = 0$
$11 \times 0 = 0$
$12 \times 0 = 0$

Exercise 4: 1a Calculate the following:

1) $3 \times 0 =$ _____

2) **1** lot of **0** is _____

3) $6 \times 0 =$ _____

4) **0** groups of **0** is _____

5) $2 \times 0 =$ _____

Score

3. Multiplication by 1

Multiplication is repeated addition.

$4 \times 1 = 4$ is the same as

$1 + 1 + 1 + 1 = 4$

$1 + 1 + 1 + 1 = 4$

For example, **four** lots of **one** flower makes **four** flowers.

If any number is multiplied by **1**, the number remains the same.

Example: | What is **8** lots of **1**?

$8 \times 1 = \bullet + \bullet + \bullet + \bullet + \bullet + \bullet + \bullet + \bullet = 8$ $8 \times 1 = 8$

$1 + 1 + 1 + 1 + 1 + 1 + 1 + 1$

Answer: **8**

Exercise 4: 1b Calculate the following:

6) **5** lots of **1** is: ♡ + ♡ + ♡ + ♡ + ♡ = _____

7) 9×1 = ⌂ + ⌂ + ⌂ + ⌂ + ⌂ + ⌂ + ⌂ + ⌂ + ⌂ = _____

8) **4** groups of **1** is: ↻ + ↻ + ↻ + ↻ = _____

9) **6** lots of **1** is: ◈ + ◈ + ◈ + ◈ + ◈ + ◈ = _____

10) 7×1 = 🛒 + 🛒 + 🛒 + 🛒 + 🛒 + 🛒 + 🛒 = _____

Note that when multiplying by **1** the number remains the same. This is the 1× table:

$0 \times 1 = 0$	$5 \times 1 = 5$	$10 \times 1 = 10$
$1 \times 1 = 1$	$6 \times 1 = 6$	$11 \times 1 = 11$
$2 \times 1 = 2$	$7 \times 1 = 7$	$12 \times 1 = 12$
$3 \times 1 = 3$	$8 \times 1 = 8$	
$4 \times 1 = 4$	$9 \times 1 = 9$	

Exercise 4: 2 Fill in the missing spaces:

Score

◉ $1 \times 1 = \underline{1}$

◉ ◉ $2 \times \underline{1} = 2$

1) ◉ ◉ ◉ $\underline{} \times 1 = 3$

2) ◉ ◉ ◉ ◉ $4 \times 1 = \underline{}$

3) ◉ ◉ ◉ ◉ ◉ $\underline{} \times 1 = 5$

4) ◉ ◉ ◉ ◉ ◉ ◉ $6 \times 1 = \underline{}$

5) ◉ ◉ ◉ ◉ ◉ ◉ ◉ $7 \times 1 = \underline{}$

6) ◉ ◉ ◉ ◉ ◉ ◉ ◉ ◉ $8 \times \underline{} = 8$

7) ◉ ◉ ◉ ◉ ◉ ◉ ◉ ◉ ◉ $\underline{} \times 1 = 9$

8) ◉ ◉ ◉ ◉ ◉ ◉ ◉ ◉ ◉ ◉ $10 \times \underline{} = 10$

9) ◉ ◉ ◉ ◉ ◉ ◉ ◉ ◉ ◉ ◉ ◉ $11 \times 1 = \underline{}$

10) ◉ ◉ ◉ ◉ ◉ ◉ ◉ ◉ ◉ ◉ ◉ ◉ $12 \times 1 = \underline{}$

4. Multiplication by 2

Multiplication is repeated addition. $3 \times 2 = 6$ is the same as $2 + 2 + 2 = 6$. The diagram below shows the repeated addition.

| 2 | 2 | 2 |

As there are **three** groups of **two** it can be written as:

$$3 \times 2 = 6$$

When multiplying, the order of the numbers does not matter, the answer is always the same.
$2 \times 3 = 6$ is the same as $3 + 3 = 6$. The diagram below shows the repeated addition.

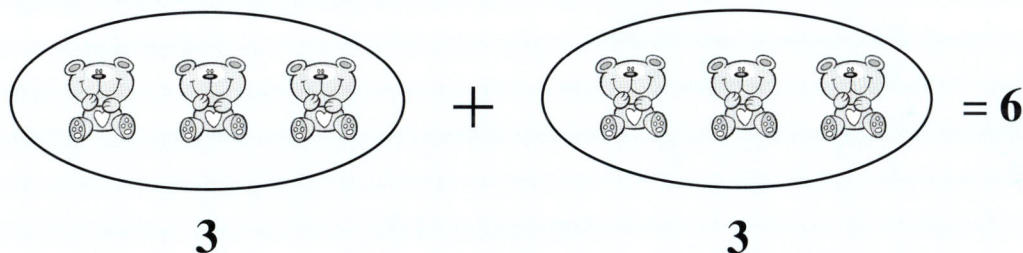

| 3 | 3 |

As there are **two** groups of **three** it can be written as:

$$2 \times 3 = 6$$

Example: | What is **5** lots of **2**?

$$5 \times 2 = \times\times + \times\times + \times\times + \times\times + \times\times = 10 \qquad 5 \times 2 = 10$$

$$2 + 2 + 2 + 2 + 2$$

Answer: **10**

Exercise 4: 3a Calculate the following:

1) **3** lots of **2** is: ⊗ + ⊗ + ⊗ = _____

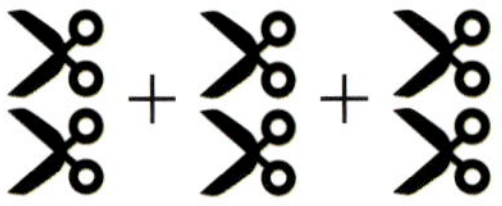

2) $6 \times 2 =$ ⊘ + ⊘ + ⊘ + ⊘ + ⊘ + ⊘ = _____

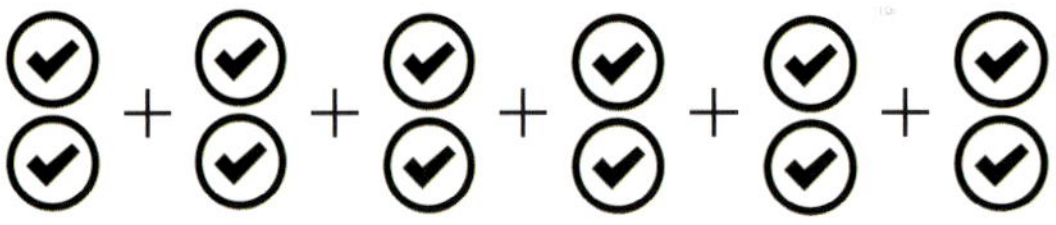

3) **7** groups of **2** is: ✈ + ✈ + ✈ + ✈ + ✈ + ✈ + ✈ = _____

4) **4** groups of **2** is: ⋀ + ⋀ + ⋀ + ⋀ = _____

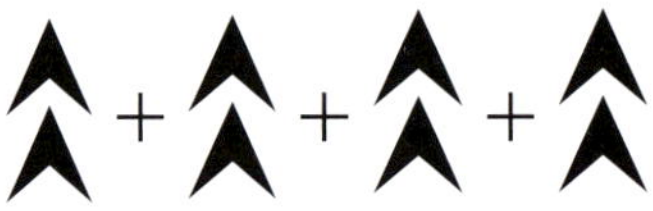

5) $8 \times 2 =$ ⌂ + ⌂ + ⌂ + ⌂ + ⌂ + ⌂ + ⌂ + ⌂ = _____

Example: | What is **2** groups of **5**?

$2 \times 5 =$ ✖✖✖ + ✖✖✖ = 10 $2 \times 5 = 10$

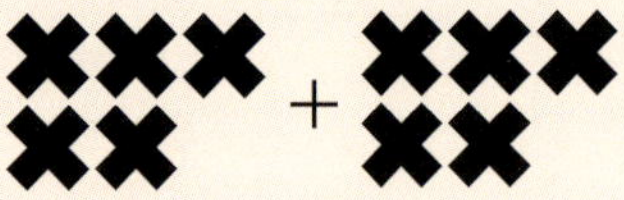

5   +   5

Answer: **10**

Exercise 4: 3b Calculate the following:

6) **2** lots of **6** is: ♋♋♋ + ♋♋♋ = _____

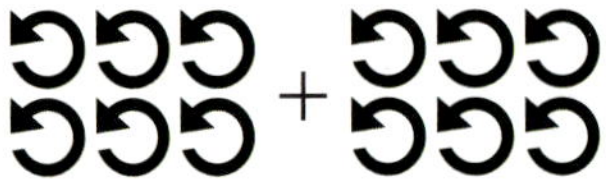

7) $2 \times 9 =$ ★★★★★ + ★★★★★ = _____

8) **2** groups of **4** is: ♫♫ + ♫♫ = _____

9) $2 \times 7 =$ 🛒🛒🛒🛒🛒🛒🛒 + 🛒🛒🛒🛒🛒🛒🛒 = _____

10) **2** lots of **3** is: ✂✂ ✂ + ✂✂ ✂ = _____

It is important to know the 2× table and be able to answer any 2× table question at random.

$0 \times 2 = 0$	$5 \times 2 = 10$	$10 \times 2 = 20$
$1 \times 2 = 2$	$6 \times 2 = 12$	$11 \times 2 = 22$
$2 \times 2 = 4$	$7 \times 2 = 14$	$12 \times 2 = 24$
$3 \times 2 = 6$	$8 \times 2 = 16$	
$4 \times 2 = 8$	$9 \times 2 = 18$	

Exercise 4: 4   Fill in the missing spaces:

$1 \times \underline{2} = 2$

$2 \times 2 = \underline{4}$

1) $\underline{} \times 2 = 6$

2) $4 \times 2 = \underline{}$

3) $\underline{} \times 2 = 10$

4) $6 \times 2 = \underline{}$

5) $7 \times 2 = \underline{}$

6) $8 \times \underline{} = 16$

7) $\underline{} \times 2 = 18$

8) $10 \times \underline{} = 20$

9) $11 \times 2 = \underline{}$

10) $12 \times 2 = \underline{}$

5. Multiplication by 3

Example: | What is **4 lots of 3**?

$4 \times 3 =$ ✓✓✓ + ✓✓✓ + ✓✓✓ + ✓✓✓ = **12**

    3 + **3** + **3** + **3**

$4 \times 3 = 12$

Answer: **12**

Exercise 4: 5a   Calculate the following:

Score

1) **2 lots of 3** is: ✂✂ + ✂✂ = _____
✂ ✂

2) $5 \times 3 =$ ᙢᙢ + ᙢᙢ + ᙢᙢ + ᙢᙢ + ᙢᙢ = _____

3) **6 groups of 3** is: ♫♩ + ♫♩ + ♫♩ + ♫♩ + ♫♩ + ♫♩ = _____

4) **3 groups of 3** is: 🛒🛒 + 🛒🛒 + 🛒🛒 = _____
🛒 🛒 🛒

5) $8 \times 3 =$ ✪✪ + ✪✪ + ✪✪ + ✪✪ + ✪✪ + ✪✪ + ✪✪ + ✪✪ = _____

Example: What is **3** groups of **5**?

$3 \times 5 =$ $= 15$ $3 \times 5 = 15$

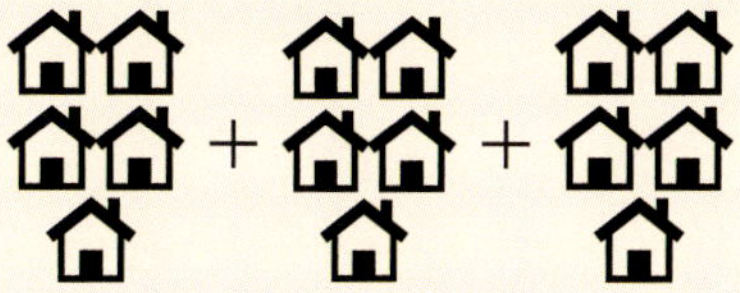

5 + 5 + 5

Answer: **15**

Exercise 4: 5b   Calculate the following:

6) **3** lots of **4** is: = _____

7) $3 \times 6 =$ = _____

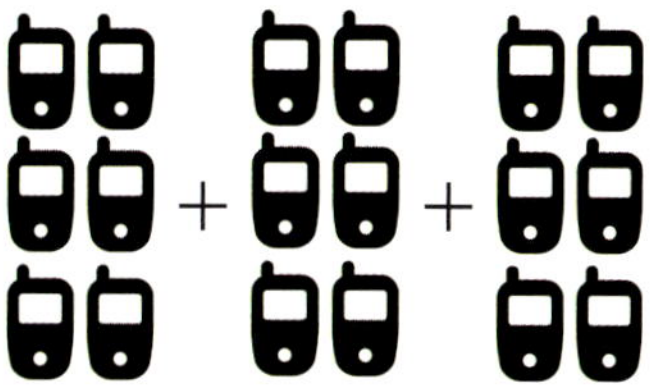

8) **3** groups of **3** is: = _____

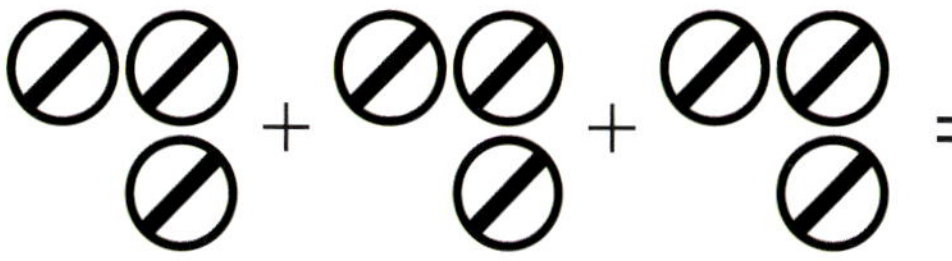

9) $3 \times 7 =$ = _____

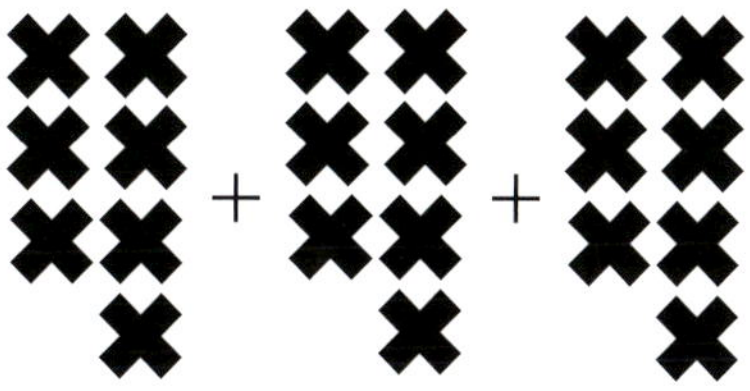

10) **3** lots of **9** is: = _____

It is important to know the 3× table and be able to answer any 3× table question at random.

$0 \times 3 = 0$	$5 \times 3 = 15$	$10 \times 3 = 30$
$1 \times 3 = 3$	$6 \times 3 = 18$	$11 \times 3 = 33$
$2 \times 3 = 6$	$7 \times 3 = 21$	$12 \times 3 = 36$
$3 \times 3 = 9$	$8 \times 3 = 24$	
$4 \times 3 = 12$	$9 \times 3 = 27$	

Exercise 4: 6   Fill in the missing spaces:

Score

$1 \times \underline{3} = 3$

$\underline{2} \times 3 = 6$

1) $3 \times 3 = \underline{}$

2) $\underline{} \times 3 = 12$

3) $5 \times 3 = \underline{}$

4) $\underline{} \times 3 = 18$

5) $7 \times \underline{} = 21$

6) $8 \times 3 = \underline{}$

7) $9 \times \underline{} = 27$

8) $\underline{} \times 3 = 30$

9) $11 \times 3 = \underline{}$

10) $12 \times \underline{} = 36$

6. Multiplication by 4

Example: What is **3** lots of **4**?

$$3 \times 4 = \boxed{} + \boxed{} + \boxed{} = 12 \qquad 3 \times 4 = 12$$

$$4 \quad + \quad 4 \quad + \quad 4$$

Answer: **12**

Exercise 4: 7a   Calculate the following:

1) **5** lots of **4** is: ⋀⋀ + ⋀⋀ + ⋀⋀ + ⋀⋀ + ⋀⋀ = _____

2) $6 \times 4 =$ ✎ + ✎ + ✎ + ✎ + ✎ + ✎ = _____

3) **7** groups of **4** is: ✕ + ✕ + ✕ + ✕ + ✕ + ✕ + ✕ = _____

4) **4** groups of **4** is: ↑↑ + ↑↑ + ↑↑ + ↑↑ = _____

5) $9 \times 4 =$ ⌂ + ⌂ + ⌂ + ⌂ + ⌂ + ⌂ + ⌂ + ⌂ + ⌂ = _____

Example: | What is **4** groups of **6**? |

$4 \times 6 =$ ⋀⋀ + ⋀⋀ + ⋀⋀ + ⋀⋀ $= 24$ $4 \times 6 = 24$

6 + 6 + 6 + 6

Answer: **24**

Exercise 4: 7b Calculate the following:

6) **4** groups of **7** is: [stars] + [stars] + [stars] + [stars] = _____

7) **4 × 3** = [symbols] + [symbols] + [symbols] + [symbols] = _____

8) **4** lots of **9** is: [notes] + [notes] + [notes] + [notes] = _____

9) **4 × 8** = [carts] + [carts] + [carts] + [carts] = _____

10) **4** lots of **5** is: [hearts] + [hearts] + [hearts] + [hearts] = _____

It is important to know the 4× table and be able to answer any 4× table question at random. The 4× table is double the 2× table, e.g. 3 × 2 = 6 and 3 × 4 = 12, 12 is double 6.

$0 \times 4 = 0$	$5 \times 4 = 20$	$10 \times 4 = 40$
$1 \times 4 = 4$	$6 \times 4 = 24$	$11 \times 4 = 44$
$2 \times 4 = 8$	$7 \times 4 = 28$	$12 \times 4 = 48$
$3 \times 4 = 12$	$8 \times 4 = 32$	
$4 \times 4 = 16$	$9 \times 4 = 36$	

Exercise 4: 8 Fill in the missing spaces:

$1 \times \underline{4} = 4$

$2 \times 4 = \underline{8}$

1) $3 \times \underline{} = 12$

2) $\underline{} \times 4 = 16$

3) $5 \times 4 = \underline{}$

4) $6 \times 4 = \underline{}$

5) $\underline{} \times 4 = 28$

6) $8 \times \underline{} = 32$

7) $9 \times 4 = \underline{}$

8) $\underline{} \times 4 = 40$

9) $11 \times \underline{} = 44$

10) $12 \times 4 = \underline{}$

7. Multiplication by 5

Example: | What is **7** lots of **5**?

$7 \times 5 = $ ♡♡♡ + ♡♡♡ + ♡♡♡ + ♡♡♡ + ♡♡♡ + ♡♡♡ + ♡♡♡ = 35

$$5 + 5 + 5 + 5 + 5 + 5 + 5$$

$$7 \times 5 = 35$$

Answer: **35**

Exercise 4: 9a Calculate the following:

1) **2** lots of **5** is: ⬆️ + ⬆️ = _____

2) **4 × 5** = ✖️ + ✖️ + ✖️ + ✖️ = _____

3) **7 × 5** = 🔧 + 🔧 + 🔧 + 🔧 + 🔧 + 🔧 + 🔧 = _____

4) **6** groups of **5** is: 🏠 + 🏠 + 🏠 + 🏠 + 🏠 + 🏠 = _____

5) **8 × 5** = ✈️ + ✈️ + ✈️ + ✈️ + ✈️ + ✈️ + ✈️ + ✈️ = _____

Example: | What is **5** groups of **8**? |

$5 \times 8 =$ ⊙ + ⊙ + ⊙ + ⊙ + ⊙ = 40 $5 \times 8 = 40$

$$8 + 8 + 8 + 8 + 8$$

Answer: **40**

Exercise 4: 9b Calculate the following:

6) $5 \times 7 =$ 🛒 + 🛒 + 🛒 + 🛒 + 🛒 = _____

7) **5** lots of **2** is: ⌃ + ⌃ + ⌃ + ⌃ + ⌃ = _____

8) **5** groups of **9** is: ⟲ + ⟲ + ⟲ + ⟲ + ⟲ = _____

9) $5 \times 6 =$ ✦ + ✦ + ✦ + ✦ + ✦ = _____

10) **5** lots of **3** is: ✂ + ✂ + ✂ + ✂ + ✂ = _____

It is important to know the 5× table and be able to answer any 5× table question at random.

$0 \times 5 = 0$	$5 \times 5 = 25$	$10 \times 5 = 50$
$1 \times 5 = 5$	$6 \times 5 = 30$	$11 \times 5 = 55$
$2 \times 5 = 10$	$7 \times 5 = 35$	$12 \times 5 = 60$
$3 \times 5 = 15$	$8 \times 5 = 40$	
$4 \times 5 = 20$	$9 \times 5 = 45$	

Exercise 4: 10 Fill in the missing spaces:

$1 \times 5 = \underline{}5$

$2 \times \underline{}5 = 10$

1) $\underline{} \times 5 = 15$

2) $4 \times \underline{} = 20$

3) $5 \times 5 = \underline{}$

4) $\underline{} \times 5 = 30$

5) $7 \times 5 = \underline{}$

6) $8 \times \underline{} = 40$

7) $9 \times 5 = \underline{}$

8) $\underline{} \times 5 = 50$

9) $11 \times \underline{} = 55$

10) $12 \times 5 = \underline{}$

8. Multiplication by 6

Example: What is **4** lots of **6**?

$4 \times 6 = $ ▦ $+$ ▦ $+$ ▦ $+$ ▦ $= 24$ $4 \times 6 = 24$

 6 $+$ 6 $+$ 6 $+$ 6

Answer: **24**

Exercise 4: 11a Calculate the following:

1) $5 \times 6 = $ ▦ $+$ ▦ $+$ ▦ $+$ ▦ $+$ ▦ $= \underline{}$

2) **4** groups of **6** is: = _____

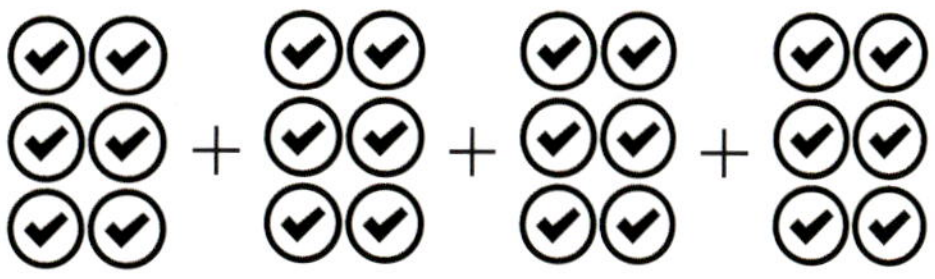

3) $6 \times 6 =$ = _____

4) $8 \times 6 =$ = _____

5) **7** lots of **6** is: = _____

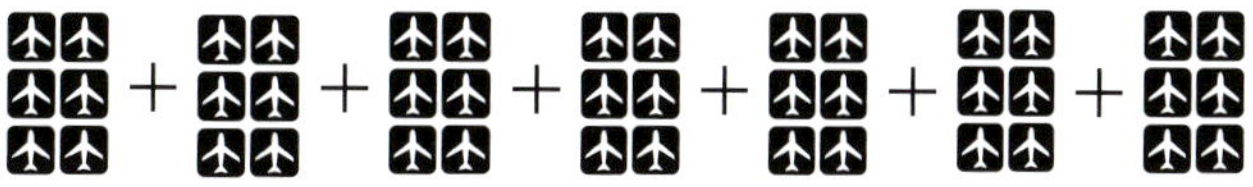

Example: | What is **6** groups of **3**? |

$6 \times 3 =$ = **18**

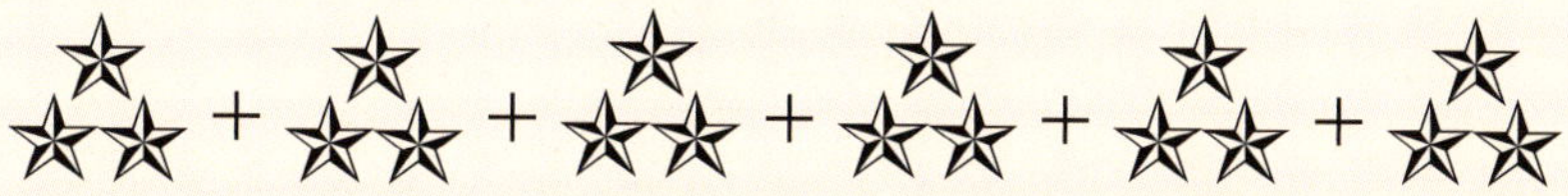

$$3 \ + \ 3 \ + \ 3 \ + \ 3 \ + \ 3 \ + \ 3$$

$$6 \times 3 = 18$$

Answer: **18**

Exercise 4: 11b Calculate the following:

6) $6 \times 8 =$ = _____

7) **6** lots of **2** is: = _____

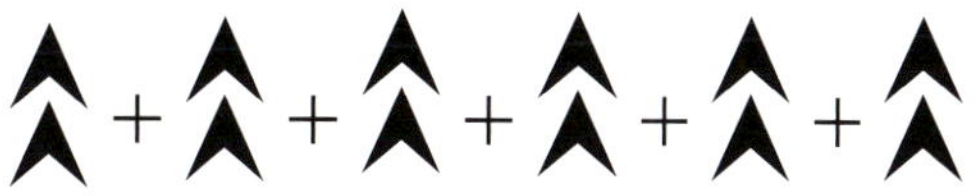

8) $6 \times 9 =$ = _____

9) $6 \times 5 =$ 🐍🐍 + 🐍🐍 + 🐍🐍 + 🐍🐍 + 🐍🐍 + 🐍🐍 = _____

10) **6 lots of 7 is:** 🛒🛒🛒 + 🛒🛒🛒 + 🛒🛒🛒 + 🛒🛒🛒 + 🛒🛒🛒 + 🛒🛒🛒 = _____

It is important to know the 6× table and be able to answer any 6× table question at random. The 6× table is double the 3× table, e.g. $5 \times 3 = 15$ and $5 \times 6 = 30$, 30 is double 15.

$0 \times 6 = 0$	$5 \times 6 = 30$	$10 \times 6 = 60$
$1 \times 6 = 6$	$6 \times 6 = 36$	$11 \times 6 = 66$
$2 \times 6 = 12$	$7 \times 6 = 42$	$12 \times 6 = 72$
$3 \times 6 = 18$	$8 \times 6 = 48$	
$4 \times 6 = 24$	$9 \times 6 = 54$	

Exercise 4: 12   Fill in the missing spaces:

Score

1) $\underline{1} \times 6 = 6$

   $2 \times \underline{6} = 12$

2) $\underline{} \times 6 = 18$

3) $4 \times 6 = \underline{}$

4) $5 \times 6 = \underline{}$

5) $6 \times \underline{} = 36$

6) $\underline{} \times 6 = 42$

7) $8 \times 6 = \underline{}$

8) $9 \times 6 = \underline{}$

9) $10 \times \underline{} = 60$

10) $\underline{} \times 6 = 66$

   $12 \times 6 = \underline{}$

9. Multiplication by 7

It is important to know the 7× table and be able to answer any 7× table question at random.

$0 \times 7 = 0$	$5 \times 7 = 35$	$10 \times 7 = 70$
$1 \times 7 = 7$	$6 \times 7 = 42$	$11 \times 7 = 77$
$2 \times 7 = 14$	$7 \times 7 = 49$	$12 \times 7 = 84$
$3 \times 7 = 21$	$8 \times 7 = 56$	
$4 \times 7 = 28$	$9 \times 7 = 63$	

Exercise 4: 13   Fill in the missing spaces:

Score

1)
2)
3)
4)
5)
6)
7)
8)
9)
10)

$1 \times 7 =$ __7__

$2 \times 7 =$ __14__

$3 \times 7 =$ ____

$4 \times 7 =$ ____

$5 \times 7 =$ ____

$6 \times 7 =$ ____

$7 \times 7 =$ ____

$8 \times 7 =$ ____

$9 \times 7 =$ ____

$10 \times 7 =$ ____

$11 \times 7 =$ ____

$12 \times 7 =$ ____

Exercise 4: 14 Fill in the missing spaces:

Score

1) $10 \times$ __ $= 70$

2) $2 \times 7 =$ ____

3) $11 \times 7 =$ ____

4) $6 \times 7 =$ ____

5) $3 \times \underline{\quad} = 21$

6) $\underline{\quad} \times 7 = 35$

7) $9 \times 7 = \underline{\quad}$

8) $7 \times 7 = \underline{\quad}$

9) $\underline{\quad} \times 7 = 56$

10) $12 \times 7 = \underline{\quad}$

10. Multiplication by 8

It is important to know the 8× table and be able to answer any 8× table question at random. The 8× table is double the 4× table, e.g. $3 \times 4 = 12$ and $3 \times 8 = 24$, 24 is double 12.

$0 \times 8 = 0$	$5 \times 8 = 40$	$10 \times 8 = 80$
$1 \times 8 = 8$	$6 \times 8 = 48$	$11 \times 8 = 88$
$2 \times 8 = 16$	$7 \times 8 = 56$	$12 \times 8 = 96$
$3 \times 8 = 24$	$8 \times 8 = 64$	
$4 \times 8 = 32$	$9 \times 8 = 72$	

Exercise 4: 15   Fill in the missing spaces:

Score

1) $1 \times 8 = \underline{8}$

2) $2 \times 8 = \underline{16}$

3) $3 \times 8 = \underline{\quad}$

4) $4 \times 8 = \underline{\quad}$

5) $5 \times 8 = \underline{\quad}$

6) $6 \times 8 = \underline{\quad}$

7) $7 \times 8 = \underline{\quad}$

8) $8 \times 8 = \underline{\quad}$

9) $9 \times 8 = \underline{\quad}$

10) $10 \times 8 = \underline{\quad}$

$11 \times 8 = \underline{\quad}$

$12 \times 8 = \underline{\quad}$

Exercise 4: 16   Fill in the missing spaces:

1) $4 \times 8 = \underline{\hspace{1cm}}$

2) $11 \times \underline{\hspace{1cm}} = 88$

3) $\underline{\hspace{1cm}} \times 8 = 16$

4) $7 \times 8 = \underline{\hspace{1cm}}$

5) $5 \times 8 = \underline{\hspace{1cm}}$

6) $1 \times \underline{\hspace{1cm}} = 8$

7) $\underline{\hspace{1cm}} \times 8 = 64$

8) $10 \times 8 = \underline{\hspace{1cm}}$

9) $12 \times 8 = \underline{\hspace{1cm}}$

10) $9 \times 8 = \underline{\hspace{1cm}}$

Score

11. Multiplication by 9

It is important to know the 9× table and be able to answer any 9× table question at random. The 9× table is triple the 3× table, e.g. $3 \times 3 = 9$ and $3 \times 9 = 27$, 27 is triple 9.

$0 \times 9 = 0$	$4 \times 9 = 36$	$7 \times 9 = 63$	$10 \times 9 = 90$
$1 \times 9 = 9$	$5 \times 9 = 45$	$8 \times 9 = 72$	$11 \times 9 = 99$
$2 \times 9 = 18$	$6 \times 9 = 54$	$9 \times 9 = 81$	$12 \times 9 = 108$
$3 \times 9 = 27$			

Exercise 4: 17   Fill in the missing spaces:

$1 \times 9 = \underline{9}$ **Score**

$2 \times 9 = \underline{18}$

1) $3 \times 9 = \underline{\hspace{1cm}}$

2) $4 \times 9 = \underline{\hspace{1cm}}$

3) $5 \times 9 = \underline{\hspace{1cm}}$

4) $6 \times 9 = \underline{\hspace{1cm}}$

5) $7 \times 9 = \underline{\hspace{1cm}}$

6) $8 \times 9 = \underline{\hspace{1cm}}$

7) $9 \times 9 = \underline{\hspace{1cm}}$

8) $10 \times 9 = \underline{\hspace{1cm}}$

9) $11 \times 9 = \underline{\hspace{1cm}}$

10) $12 \times 9 = \underline{\hspace{1cm}}$

Exercise 4: 18   Fill in the missing spaces:

1) $2 \times \underline{\hspace{1cm}} = 18$

2) $10 \times 9 = \underline{\hspace{1cm}}$

3) $8 \times \underline{\hspace{1cm}} = 72$

4) $4 \times 9 = \underline{\hspace{1cm}}$

5) $\underline{\hspace{1cm}} \times 9 = 9$

6) $3 \times \underline{\hspace{1cm}} = 27$

7) $7 \times 9 = \underline{\hspace{1cm}}$

8) $\underline{\hspace{1cm}} \times 9 = 45$

9) $\underline{\hspace{1cm}} \times 9 = 81$

10) $\underline{\hspace{1cm}} \times 9 = 108$

12. Multiplication by 10

Example: | What is **3** lots of **10**?

$3 \times 10 = $ $ = 30$ $3 \times 10 = 30$

$$10 \quad + \quad 10 \quad + \quad 10$$

Answer: **30**

Exercise 4: 19a   Calculate the following:

1) **5** lots of **10** is: $= \underline{\hspace{1cm}}$

2) $7 \times 10 = $ $= \underline{\hspace{1cm}}$

3) $6 \times 10 =$ ⣿ $+$ ⣿ $+$ ⣿ $+$ ⣿ $+$ ⣿ $+$ ⣿ $=$ _____

4) **4** groups of **10** is: ⣿ $+$ ⣿ $+$ ⣿ $+$ ⣿ $=$ _____

5) $8 \times 10 =$ ⣿ $+$ ⣿ $+$ ⣿ $+$ ⣿ $+$ ⣿ $+$ ⣿ $+$ ⣿ $+$ ⣿ $=$ _____

Example: | What is **10** groups of **4**? |

$10 \times 4 = \left(\vdots\right) + \left(\vdots\right) + \left(\vdots\right) + \left(\vdots\right) + \left(\vdots\right) + \left(\vdots\right) + \left(\vdots\right) + \left(\vdots\right) + \left(\vdots\right) + \left(\vdots\right) = 40$

$$4 + 4 + 4 + 4 + 4 + 4 + 4 + 4 + 4 + 4$$

$$10 \times 4 = 40$$

Answer: **40**

Exercise 4: 19b Calculate the following:

6) **10** lots of **2** is: ⠿ $+$ ⠿ $+$ ⠿ $+$ ⠿ $+$ ⠿ $+$ ⠿ $+$ ⠿ $+$ ⠿ $+$ ⠿ $+$ ⠿

= _____

7) $10 \times 7 =$ ⣿ $+$ ⣿ $+$ ⣿ $+$ ⣿ $+$ ⣿ $+$ ⣿ $+$ ⣿ $+$ ⣿ $+$ ⣿ $+$ ⣿

= _____

8) **10** groups of **5** is: ⣿ $+$ ⣿ $+$ ⣿ $+$ ⣿ $+$ ⣿ $+$ ⣿ $+$ ⣿ $+$ ⣿ $+$ ⣿ $+$ ⣿

= _____

9) $10 \times 8 =$ ⣿ + ⣿ + ⣿ + ⣿ + ⣿ + ⣿ + ⣿ + ⣿ + ⣿ + ⣿

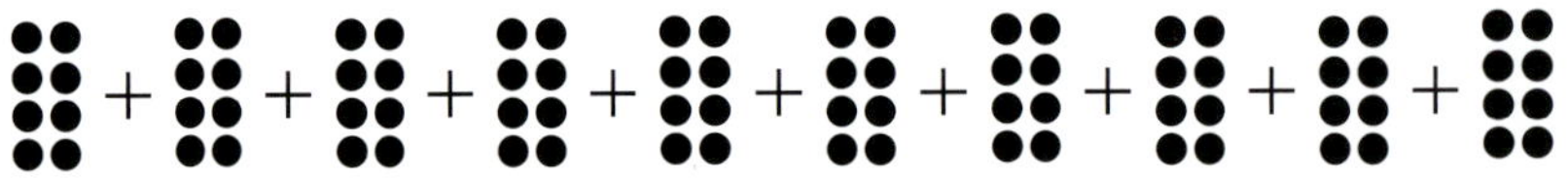

       = _____

10) **10** lots of **9** is: ⣿ + ⣿ + ⣿ + ⣿ + ⣿ + ⣿ + ⣿ + ⣿ + ⣿ + ⣿

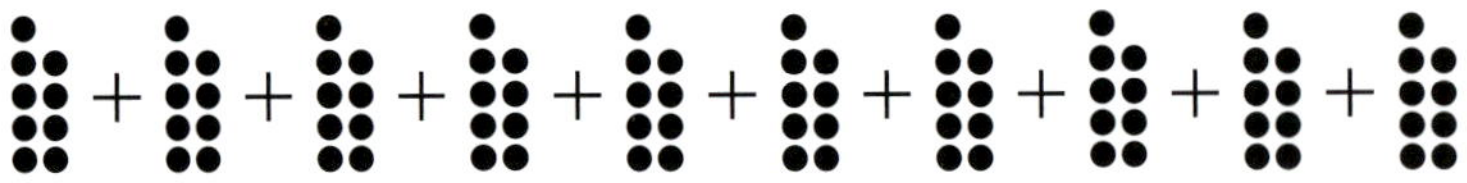

       = _____

It is important to know the 10× table and be able to answer any 10× table question at random. The 10× table is double the 5× table, e.g. $4 \times 5 = 20$ and $4 \times 10 = 40$, 40 is double 20.

$0 \times 10 = 0$	$5 \times 10 = 50$	$10 \times 10 = 100$
$1 \times 10 = 10$	$6 \times 10 = 60$	$11 \times 10 = 110$
$2 \times 10 = 20$	$7 \times 10 = 70$	$12 \times 10 = 120$
$3 \times 10 = 30$	$8 \times 10 = 80$	
$4 \times 10 = 40$	$9 \times 10 = 90$	

Exercise 4: 20   Fill in the missing spaces:

Score

1) $\underline{1} \times 10 = 10$

2) $2 \times \underline{10} = 20$

3) $\underline{} \times 10 = 30$

4) $4 \times 10 = \underline{}$

5) $5 \times 10 = \underline{}$

6) $6 \times \underline{} = 60$

7) $\underline{} \times 10 = 70$

8) $8 \times 10 = \underline{}$

9) $\underline{} \times 10 = 90$

10) $10 \times 10 = \underline{}$

$11 \times \underline{} = 110$

$12 \times 10 = \underline{}$

Multiplying by multiples of **10** is very easy to do.

To multiply by **10**, put one **zero (0)** on the end.

$2 \times 10 = 20$

U
2

$\xrightarrow{\times 10}$

T	U
2	0

To multiply by **100**, put two **zeros (00)** on the end.

$2 \times 100 = 200$

U
2

$\xrightarrow{\times 100}$

H	T	U
2	0	0

To multiply by **1,000**, put three **zeros (000)** on the end.

$2 \times 1,000 = 2,000$

U
2

$\xrightarrow{\times 1,000}$

Th	H	T	U
2	0	0	0

Example: | Calculate **36 × 100**. |

Count the number of zeros on the multiplying number and write the same number of zeros on the number to be multiplied. **36** with two zeros written at the end will become **3,600**.

$$36 \times 100 = 3,600$$

Answer: **3,600**

Exercise 4: 21   Calculate the following:

1) $4 \times 10 =$ _____

2) $19 \times 10 =$ _____

3) $184 \times 10 =$ _____

4) $62 \times 100 =$ _____

5) $99 \times 100 =$ _____

6) $207 \times 100 =$ _____

7) $3 \times 1,000 =$ _____

8) $51 \times 1,000 =$ _____

9) $739 \times 1,000 =$ _____

10) $485 \times 1,000 =$ _____

Score

13. Multiplication by 11

It is important to know the 11× table and be able to answer any 11× table question at random.

$$0 \times 11 = 0 \qquad 5 \times 11 = 55 \qquad 10 \times 11 = 110$$
$$1 \times 11 = 11 \qquad 6 \times 11 = 66 \qquad 11 \times 11 = 121$$
$$2 \times 11 = 22 \qquad 7 \times 11 = 77 \qquad 12 \times 11 = 132$$
$$3 \times 11 = 33 \qquad 8 \times 11 = 88$$
$$4 \times 11 = 44 \qquad 9 \times 11 = 99$$

Note: It is easy to remember the 11× table.

- Repeat the digit of the number being multiplied up to 9×, e.g. $3 \times 11 = 33$ (3 is repeated to make **33**).

- For 10×, 11× and 12× simply place the digits **1**, **2** and **3** in between the multiplier to give the answer.

$$10 \times 11 = 1\underline{1}0 \qquad 11 \times 11 = 1\underline{2}1 \qquad 12 \times 11 = 1\underline{3}2$$

Exercise 4: 22   Fill in the missing spaces:

Score

	$1 \times 11 = $	11
	$2 \times 11 = $	22
1)	$3 \times 11 = $	___
2)	$4 \times 11 = $	___
3)	$5 \times 11 = $	___
4)	$6 \times 11 = $	___
5)	$7 \times 11 = $	___
6)	$8 \times 11 = $	___
7)	$9 \times 11 = $	___
8)	$10 \times 11 = $	___
9)	$11 \times 11 = $	___
10)	$12 \times 11 = $	___

Exercise 4: 23 Fill in the missing spaces:

1) $1 \times \underline{} = 11$
2) $7 \times 11 = \underline{}$
3) $9 \times \underline{} = 99$
4) $\underline{} \times 11 = 66$
5) $\underline{} \times 11 = 22$
6) $\underline{} \times 11 = 110$
7) $8 \times 11 = \underline{}$
8) $4 \times \underline{} = 44$
9) $12 \times 11 = \underline{}$
10) $11 \times 11 = \underline{}$

14. Multiplication by 12

It is important to know the 12× table and be able to answer any 12× table question at random. The 12× table is double the 6× table, e.g. $3 \times 6 = 18$ and $3 \times 12 = 36$, 36 is double 18.

$0 \times 12 = 0$	$4 \times 12 = 48$	$7 \times 12 = 84$	$10 \times 12 = 120$
$1 \times 12 = 12$	$5 \times 12 = 60$	$8 \times 12 = 96$	$11 \times 12 = 132$
$2 \times 12 = 24$	$6 \times 12 = 72$	$9 \times 12 = 108$	$12 \times 12 = 144$
$3 \times 12 = 36$			

Exercise 4: 24 Fill in the missing spaces:

$1 \times 12 = \underline{12}$
$2 \times 12 = \underline{24}$
3) $3 \times 12 = \underline{}$
4) $4 \times 12 = \underline{}$
5) $5 \times 12 = \underline{}$
6) $6 \times 12 = \underline{}$
7) $7 \times 12 = \underline{}$
8) $8 \times 12 = \underline{}$
9) $9 \times 12 = \underline{}$
10) $10 \times 12 = \underline{}$
$11 \times 12 = \underline{}$
$12 \times 12 = \underline{}$

Exercise 4: 25 Fill in the missing spaces:

1) $2 \times 12 =$ ____

2) ___ $\times 12 = 48$

3) $7 \times 12 =$ ____

4) $5 \times 12 =$ ____

5) ___ $\times 12 = 96$

6) $6 \times$ ___ $= 72$

7) $9 \times 12 =$ ____

8) $11 \times 12 =$ ____

9) $10 \times$ ___ $= 120$

10) $12 \times 12 =$ ____

15. Multiplication Squares

Multiplication Squares (Times Tables Boxes) are useful for reinforcing times tables knowledge. Filling in the boxes will aid the learning of times tables in a random manner.

Example: Fill in the times tables box.

×	5	6	7	8	9
5					
6					

To fill in the box, the first number in the first row is multiplied by the first number in the first column.

This would be $5 \times 5 = 25$

This step is then repeated along all of the columns and rows, for example, $9 \times 6 = 54$

The completed box shows part of the $5\times$ and $6\times$ tables.

×	5	6	7	8	9
5	25				
6					54

×	5	6	7	8	9
5	25	30	35	40	45
6	30	36	42	48	54

Exercise 4: 26 Complete the box:

×	2	3	4	5	6	7	8	9	10	11	12
2	4	6	8	10	12	14	16	18	20	22	24
1) 3											
2) 4											
3) 5											
4) 6											
5) 7											
6) 8											
7) 9											
8) 10											
9) 11											
10) 12											

Score

Exercise 4: 27 Complete the box:

×	3	8	11	6	4	9	12	2	10	7	5
2	6	16	22	12	8	18	24	4	20	14	10
1) 7											
2) 4											
3) 10											
4) 6											
5) 3											
6) 9											
7) 11											
8) 5											
9) 12											
10) 8											

Score

16. Number Sentences

Exercise 4: 28   Fill in the missing spaces:

Score

1) $7 \times 5 =$ _____

2) $8 \times 6 =$ _____

3) $2 \times 0 =$ _____

4) $9 \times 12 =$ _____

5) $8 \times 7 =$ _____

6) $4 \times 6 =$ _____

7) $3 \times 9 =$ _____

8) $7 \times 4 =$ _____

9) $2 \times 6 =$ _____

10) $5 \times 11 =$ _____

Exercise 4: 29   Fill in the missing spaces:

Score

1) $8 \times 12 =$ _____

2) $7 \times$ _____ $= 0$

3) _____ $\times 3 = 21$

4) $7 \times 6 =$ _____

5) $6 \times$ _____ $= 24$

6) $4 \times 11 =$ _____

7) _____ $\times 10 = 100$

8) $6 \times$ _____ $= 72$

9) $8 \times$ _____ $= 56$

10) _____ $\times 9 = 54$

17. Partitioning

Partitioning means to break up numbers into smaller parts, making calculations easier. It is useful when multiplying numbers larger than **12**.

For example, **24** can be partitioned into **20** and **4** (**2** tens and **4** units).

Example: | Calculate **17 × 5**. |

Step 1 - Split the first number: $17 = 10$ and 7

Step 2 - Multiply the ten: $10 \times 5 = 50$

Step 3 - Multiply the units: $7 \times 5 = 35$

Step 4 - Add the answers together: $50 + 35 = 85$

This can be shown on a number line:

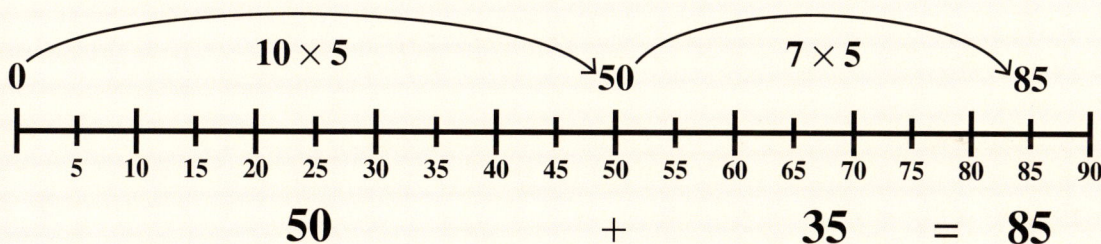

$$10 \times 5 \qquad 7 \times 5$$

0   50   85

5   10   15   20   25   30   35   40   45   50   55   60   65   70   75   80   85   90

50   +   **35**   =   **85**

Answer: **85**

Exercise 4: 30   Calculate the following:

Score

1) 16×3

     $16 = [\underline{\;10\;} \, \& \, \underline{\;6\;}]$

     $\underline{\;10\;} \times \underline{\;3\;} = \underline{\;30\;}$

     $\underline{\;6\;} \times \underline{\;3\;} = \underline{\;18\;}$

     $\underline{\;30\;} + \underline{\;18\;} = \underline{\qquad}$

2) 13×9

     $13 = [\underline{\;10\;} \, \& \, \underline{\;3\;}]$

     $\underline{\;10\;} \times \underline{\;9\;} = \underline{\;90\;}$

     $\underline{\;3\;} \times \underline{\;9\;} = \underline{\;27\;}$

     $\underline{\;90\;} + \underline{\;27\;} = \underline{\qquad}$

3) **18 × 4**

   18 = [_10_ & _8_]

   _10_ × _4_ = _____

   _8_ × _4_ = ____

   _____ + ____ = _____

4) **13 × 5**

   13 = [_10_ & _3_]

   _10_ × _5_ = _____

   _3_ × _5_ = ____

   _____ + ____ = _____

5) **18 × 6**

   18 = [____ & ____]

   ___ × _6_ = ____

   ___ × _6_ = ____

   _____ + ____ = _____

6) **15 × 9**

   15 = [____ & ____]

   ___ × _9_ = _____

   ___ × _9_ = ____

   _____ + ____ = _____

7) **14 × 7**

   14 = [____ & ____]

   ___ × ___ = _____

   ___ × ___ = ____

   _____ + ____ = _____

8) **19 × 2**

   19 = [____ & ____]

   ___ × ___ = _____

   ___ × ___ = ____

   _____ + ____ = _____

9) **14 × 8**

   14 = [____ & ____]

   ___ × ___ = ____

   ___ × ___ = ____

   _____ + ____ = _____

10) **16 × 7**

   16 = [____ & ____]

   ___ × ___ = ____

   ___ × ___ = ____

   _____ + ____ = _____

18. Short Multiplication

Multiplication can be shown horizontally or in a linear format, for example:

U   U   Units

$$3 \times 2 = 6$$

Units

$$\begin{array}{r} 3 \\ 2 \times \\ \hline 6 \\ \hline \end{array}$$

For calculation purposes it is normally shown in vertical or column format.

There are two main methods for short multiplication using columns:

- Expanded Short Multiplication
- Standard Short Multiplication

a. Expanded Short Multiplication

Expanded Short Multiplication involves multiplying each column individually and then totalling the answers, without the need to carry.

It is useful to know this technique, but standard short multiplication is a more efficient method and will be explained later.

Example: Calculate **632 × 7**.

Each digit of the number being multiplied is multiplied separately, beginning with the units.

Step 1 - Multiply the units column.

     2 units × **7** units = **14** units

     This is **1** ten and **4** units.

H   T   U

$$\begin{array}{r} 6\ 3\ 2 \\ 7 \times \\ \hline 1\ 4 \\ \hline \end{array}$$

Step 2 - Multiply the tens column.

3 tens × 7 units = **21** tens

This is the same as **210** units, so place a zero in the units column.

$$
\begin{array}{r}
\text{H} \ \text{T} \ \text{U} \\
6 \ \boxed{3} \ 2 \\
\boxed{7} \times \\
\hline
1 \ 4 \\
\hline
2 \ 1 \ 0
\end{array}
$$

Step 3 - Multiply the hundreds column.

6 hundreds × 7 units = **42** hundreds

This is the same as **4,200** units, so place zeros in the tens and units columns.

$$
\begin{array}{r}
\text{Th} \ \text{H} \ \text{T} \ \text{U} \\
\boxed{6} \ 3 \ 2 \\
\boxed{7} \times \\
\hline
1 \ 4 \\
\hline
2 \ 1 \ 0 \\
\hline
4 \ 2 \ 0 \ 0
\end{array}
$$

Step 4 - Add the answers together.

14 + 210 + 4,200 = **4,424**

$$
\begin{array}{r}
\text{Th} \ \text{H} \ \text{T} \ \text{U} \\
6 \ 3 \ 2 \\
7 \times \\
\hline
1 \ 4 \\
2 \ 1 \ 0 \\
4 \ 2 \ 0 \ 0 \\
\hline
4 \ 4 \ 2 \ 4
\end{array}
$$

Answer: **4,424**

Exercise 4: 31   Calculate the following:

1) **297**
   6 ×
     42
   540
  1200

2) **765**
   3 ×
     15
   180
  2100

3) **481**
   7 ×
      7
   560

4) **133**
   4 ×
     12

5) **583**
   8 ×

6) **696**
   2 ×

7) **387**
   5 ×

8) **805**
   9 ×

9) **963**
   7 ×

10) **618**
    4 ×

Score

b. Standard Short Multiplication

Standard Short Multiplication involves multiplying each column individually, carrying the hundreds and tens and writing the answers on one line.

This is the most commonly used method as it is quicker.

(i) One-digit Column Multiplication

Example: Calculate **6 × 2.**

Step 1 - Multiply the units column.

$6 × 2 = 12$ units

This is split into **2** units and **1** ten, which is carried.

```
  T U
    6
    2 ×
  ___
    2
  1
```

Step 2 - As there are no tens to multiply, the **1** carried ten is moved into the tens answer column.

```
  T U
    6
    2 ×
  ___
  1 2
  ___
```

Answer: **12**

Exercise 4: 32 Calculate the following:

1)   **9**
     4 ×
_____

2)   **9**
     2 ×
_____

3)   **6**
     6 ×
_____

4)   **7**
     2 ×
_____

(ii) Two-digit Column Multiplication

Example: Calculate 32×5.

Step 1 - Multiply the units column.

$2 \times 5 = 10$ units

This is split into **0** units and **1** ten, which is carried.

$$\begin{array}{cc} \text{T} & \text{U} \\ 3 & 2 \\ & 5 \times \\ \hline & 0 \\ 1 & \end{array}$$

Step 2 - Multiply the tens column.
$3 \times 5 = 15$ tens

Add the **1** carried ten to give **16** tens.

This is split into **6** tens and **1** hundred, which are carried.

$$\begin{array}{ccc} \text{H} & \text{T} & \text{U} \\ & 3 & 2 \\ & & 5 \times \\ \hline & 6 & 0 \\ 1 & 1 & \end{array}$$

Step 3 - As there are no hundreds to multiply, the **1** carried hundred is moved into the hundreds answer column.

$$\begin{array}{ccc} \text{H} & \text{T} & \text{U} \\ & 3 & 2 \\ & & 5 \times \\ \hline 1 & 6 & 0 \\ 1 & 1 & \end{array}$$

Answer: **160**

Exercise 4: 33   Calculate the following:

1)
$$97$$
$$7 \times$$
_____

2)
$$36$$
$$2 \times$$
_____

3)
$$58$$
$$5 \times$$
_____

4)
$$74$$
$$8 \times$$
_____

5)
$$19$$
$$3 \times$$
_____

6)
$$23$$
$$9 \times$$
_____

7)
$$45$$
$$4 \times$$
_____

8)
$$68$$
$$6 \times$$
_____

9)
$$82$$
$$9 \times$$
_____

10)
$$49$$
$$8 \times$$
_____

Score

(iii) Three-digit Column Multiplication

Example: Calculate 235×4.

Step 1 - Multiply the units column.

$5 \times 4 = 20$ units

This is split into **0** units and **2** tens, which are carried.

$$\begin{array}{r} \text{H T U} \\ 2\,3\,5 \\ 4 \times \\ \hline 0 \\ \hline {\scriptstyle 2} \end{array}$$

Step 2 - Multiply the tens column.

$$3 \times 4 = 12 \text{ tens}$$

Add the **2** carried tens to give **14** tens.

This is split into **4** tens and **1** hundred, which is carried.

```
  H T U
  2 3 5
      4 ×
  ─────
    4 0
  ─────
  1 2
```

Step 3 - Multiply the hundreds column.

$$2 \times 4 = 8 \text{ hundreds}$$

Add the **1** carried hundred to give **9** hundreds.

```
  H T U
  2 3 5
      4 ×
  ─────
  9 4 0
  ─────
  1 2
```

Answer: **940**

Exercise 4: 34   Calculate the following:

1)
```
  1 8 3
      9 ×
  ─────
  ─────
```

2)
```
  6 2 4
      3 ×
  ─────
  ─────
```

3)
```
  9 3 2
      8 ×
  ─────
  ─────
```

4)
```
  4 6 2
      2 ×
  ─────
  ─────
```

5)
```
  2 1 3
      6 ×
  ─────
  ─────
```

6)
```
  3 7 9
      4 ×
  ─────
  ─────
```

7) 578
   $7 \times$ _____
   _____

8) 793
   $3 \times$ _____
   _____

9) 815
   $5 \times$ _____
   _____

10) 989
    $6 \times$ _____
    _____

19. Multiplication in Words

There are many different terms for multiplication.
Here is a list of the most commonly used terms:

- Find the product of
- Scale up by
- Repeated Addition
- Multiply
- Times
- Number of sets/groups/lots of
- Double/Twice (multiply by **2**)
- Treble/Triple (multiply by **3**)
- Quadruple (multiply by **4**)
- **7** × **3** can be written as **7 threes**

Example: Find the product of **four hundred and ninety-eight** and **five**.

Convert the words into a number sentence. 'Find the product' is the same thing as using the × sign between the numbers.

$$498 \times 5$$

Solve by using standard short multiplication.

```
  4 9 8
    5 ×
─────────
2 4 9 0
  4 4
```

Answer: **2,490**

Exercise 4: 35 Answer the following:

1) Find the product of **three hundred and forty-one** and **seven**. _____

2) Scale up **five hundred and fifty-two** by **nine**. _____

3) Triple **nine hundred and fifty-nine**. _____

4) Times **one hundred and seventy-eight** by **six**. _____

5) Quadruple **three hundred and ninety-five**. _____

6) What is **811 fives**? _____

7) Double **six hundred and thirty-two**. _____

8) What is **seven hundred and forty-eight** groups of **eight**? _____

9) Multiply **four hundred and forty-two** by **nine**. _____

10) Scale up **two hundred and thirty-seven** by **six**. _____

Score

20. Problem Solving

Example: | Natalie planted **7** rows of carrots, with **18** in each row. If **37** carrots were destroyed by frost, how many carrots were left?

Step 1 - Multiply to find the total number of carrots. Convert the problem into a number sentence:

$18 \times 7 = 126$

$$\begin{array}{r} 18 \\ 7 \times \\ \hline 126 \\ {\scriptstyle 5} \end{array}$$

Step 2 - Subtract to find the left over carrots. The number sentence is:

$126 - 37 = 89$

$$\begin{array}{r} \overset{0}{\cancel{1}}\overset{11}{2}\overset{1}{6} \\ 37 - \\ \hline 89 \end{array}$$

Answer: **89 carrots**

Exercise 4: 36   Answer the following:

1) There are **twelve** children in a group. **Seven** have **twelve** trading cards each and the rest have **eight** each. How many cards does the group have in total? _____

2) Eva has **six** email accounts, which each receive **21** emails per day. How many emails does Eva receive in total each day? _____

3) Adam has **two** pieces of fruit every day for lunch. Chloe has **three** pieces of fruit every day for lunch. In total, how many pieces of fruit do they have over **five** days? _____

4) David has **4** aunts who each have **two** children. How many cousins does David have in total? _____

5) Sheila has **nine** packs of sweets. Each pack has **62** sweets. Sheila eats **12** sweets. How many sweets does she have left over? _____

6) On a bus there are **twelve** rows on each side with **2** seats per row. There are a total of **10** seats which cannot be sat in. How many seats can be filled? _____

7) Each desk has **one** pen, **one** pencil and **one** highlighter on it. If there are **12** desks in a room, how many pieces of stationery are there? _____

8) A skyscraper has **six** flats on each floor. There are **32** floors. How many flats are there in total? _____

9) A chocolate bar is made up of **four** rows of **four** squares. How many squares of chocolate are there altogether in **nine** bars of chocolate? _____

10) There is a group of **124 seven-year-olds**. What is their combined total age? _____

Score

Chapter Five
DIVISION
1. Division Terms

Division is the opposite or inverse of multiplication. It is the process of sharing or splitting a number into equal parts.

For example:
If there are **6** marbles in a bag to be shared between **3** children, each child will receive **2** marbles.

This is often represented in a number sentence, such as:

$$6 \div 3 = 2$$

This symbol means 'divide by'

The answer is called the 'quotient'

Division is repeated subtraction.

For example: $6 \div 3 = 2$ is the same as $6 - 3 - 3 = 0$. As **2** lots of **3** make **6**, the answer is **2**.

Division calculations do not give the same answer when written the other way round:

$6 \div 3 = 2$, but $3 \div 6$ does not equal **2**.

If a number divides exactly it is said to be **divisible**.

2. Division by 0

It is not possible to divide by **0**. This is because division means to split something into equal parts or groups.

If the **6** sweets are divided among **zero** children, how many sweets will each child receive?

$$\div \textbf{ no children}$$

$$6 \div 0$$

This does not make sense.

As there are no children, it is not possible to answer this question.

3. Division by 1

Division is repeated subtraction. $3 \div 1 = 3$ is the same as $3 - 1 - 1 - 1 = 0$.

For example, **three** flowers subtract **three** flowers gives **zero** flowers.

$$- \quad - \quad - \quad = 0$$

$$3 - 1 - 1 - 1 = 0$$

If a number is divided by **1** the number remains the same.

Example: Calculate $4 \div$ _____ $= 4$.

When the answer in a division calculation is the same as the original number, the number must have been divided by **1**.

Answer: $4 \div 1 = 4$

Exercise 5: 1 Calculate the following:

1) $5 \div 1 =$ _____

2) _____ $\div 1 = 2$

3) $6 \div$ _____ $= 6$

4) $9 \div 1 =$ _____

5) _____ $\div 1 = 7$

6) $8 \div$ _____ $= 8$

7) $3 \div 1$ is the same as $3 -$ __1__ $-$ __1__ $-$ __1__ $=$ ____

8) $2 \div 1$ is the same as $2 -$ ____ $-$ ____ $=$ ____

9) $1 - 1 = 0$ is the same as ____ $\div$ ____ $=$ ____

10) $4 - 1 - 1 - 1 - 1 = 0$ is the same as ____ $\div$ ____ $=$ ____

4. Division by 2

Division means to share out something equally.

For example:

There are **10** items. If these are shared out into **2** groups, there will be **5** items in each group.

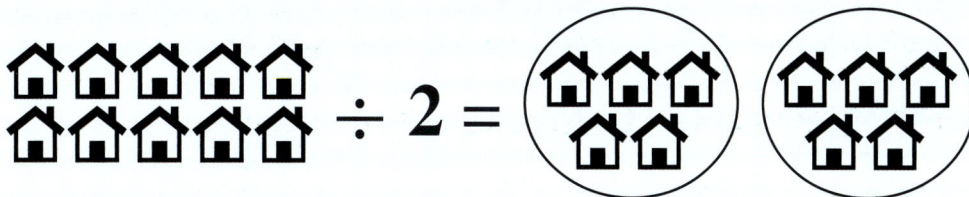

This can be written as:

$$10 \div 2 = 5$$

Example: $\boxed{\text{Calculate } 8 \div 2.}$

When dividing by **2**, the number is being shared or split into **two** groups.

8 shared out between **two** groups means there are **4** in each group.

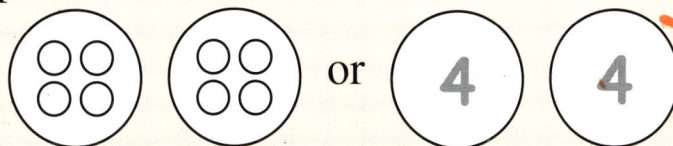

Answer: $8 \div 2 = 4$

Exercise 5: 2 Calculate the following:

1) $6 \div 2 = $ _____

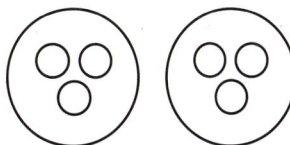

2) $16 \div 2 = $ _____

3) $4 \div 2 =$ _____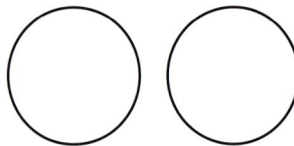

4) $12 \div 2 =$ _____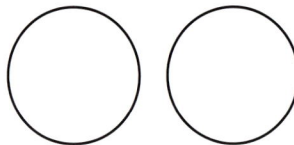

5) $20 \div 2 =$ _____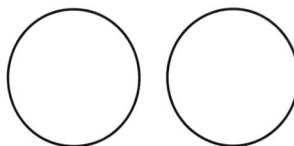

6) $2 \div 2 =$ _____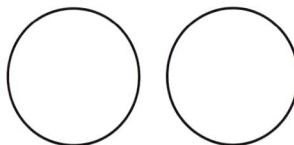

7) $18 \div 2 =$ _____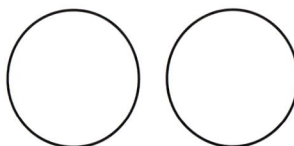

8) $22 \div 2 =$ _____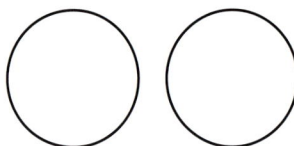

9) $14 \div 2 =$ _____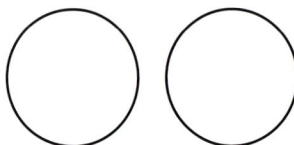

10) $24 \div 2 =$ _____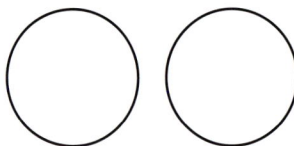

Division is the inverse or opposite of multiplication.

This means that knowledge of the times tables up to 12× is very useful for division calculations.

For example:

If there are **6** lots of **2** toys, this means there are **12** toys in total.

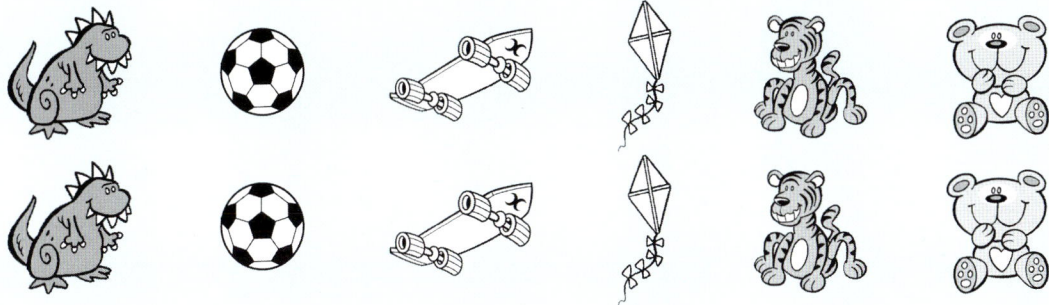

$$6 \times 2 = 12$$

If these **12** toys are shared out between **6** children, each child will receive **2** toys.

$$12 \div 6 = 2$$

The **12** toys could also be shared out between **2** children, then each child will receive **6** toys.

$$12 \div 2 = 6$$

This relationship can be shown as a times table triangle. Every multiplication calculation contains two division calculations, as division is the inverse or opposite of multiplication.

12

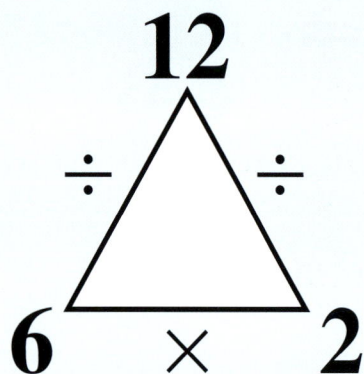

The three calculations shown on this triangle are:

$$12 \div 6 = 2$$
$$12 \div 2 = 6$$
$$6 \times 2 = 12$$

Example: | Complete the times table triangle.

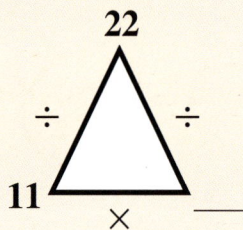

Divide the top number by the number on the left-hand side of the triangle.

$$22 \div 11 = 2$$

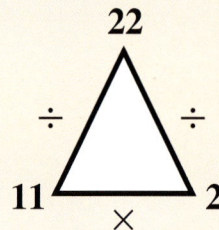

Exercise 5: 3   Complete the times tables triangle:

1)

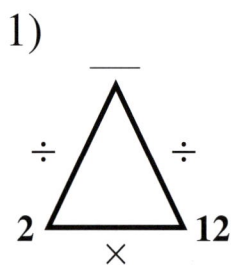

2)   12

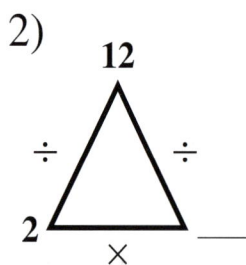

3)

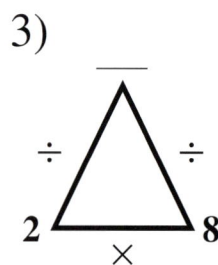

4)   14

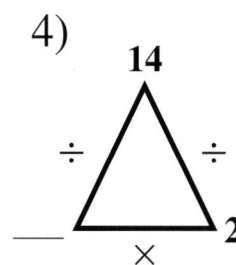

5)   6

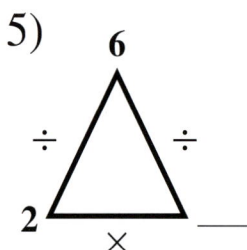

6)   2

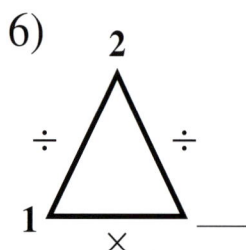

7)

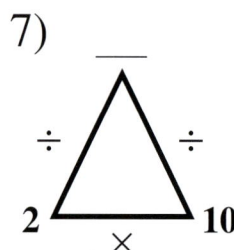

8)   4

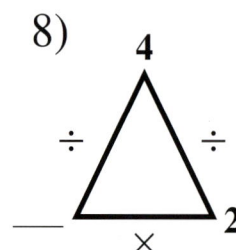

9) 10

$\div$ △ $\div$

___ × 2

10) ___

$\div$ △ $\div$

2 × 4

Score

5. Division by 3

Division means to share out something equally.

For example:

There are **12** symbols. If these are shared out between **3** children, they will each have **4** symbols.

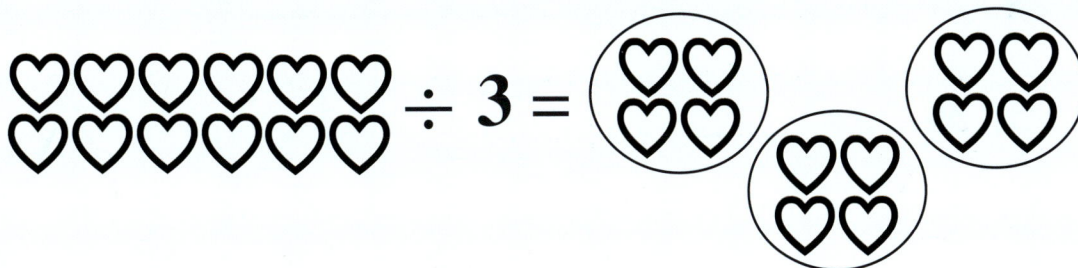

This can be written as:

$$12 \div 3 = 4$$

Example: Calculate $15 \div 3$.

When dividing by **3**, the number is being shared or split into **three** groups.

15 shared out between **three** groups means there are **5** in each group.

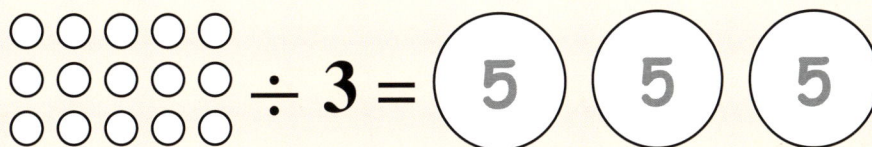

Answer: $15 \div 3 = 5$

Exercise 5: 4 Calculate the following:

1) $24 \div 3 =$ _____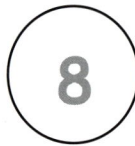

2) $0 \div 3 =$ _____

3) $27 \div 3 =$ _____

4) $9 \div 3 =$ _____

5) $36 \div 3 =$ _____

6) $6 \div 3 =$ _____

7) $18 \div 3 =$ _____

8) $30 \div 3 =$ _____

9) $3 \div 3 =$ _____

10) $21 \div 3 =$ _____

Score

Example: Complete the times table triangle.

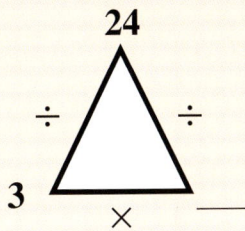

Divide the top number by the number on the left-hand side of the triangle.

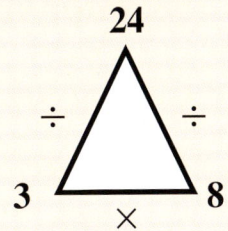

$$24 \div 3 = 8$$

Exercise 5: 5   Complete the times tables triangle:

1)
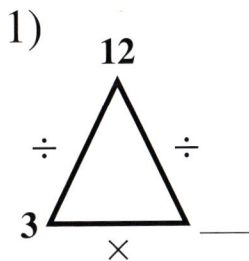

2)
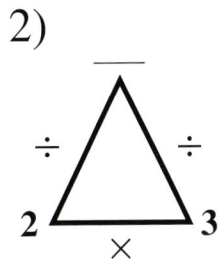

3)
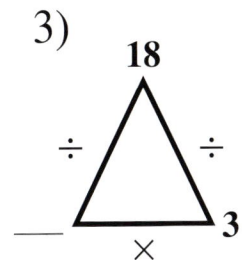

4)
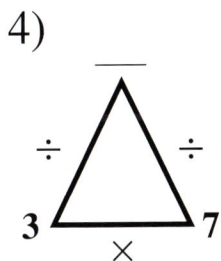

5)
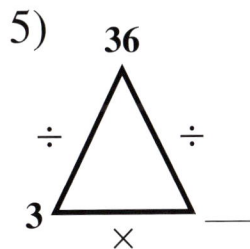

6)
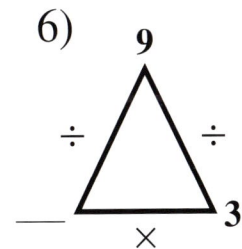

7)
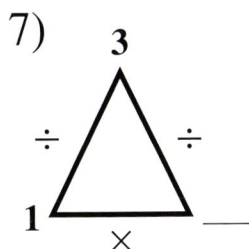

8)
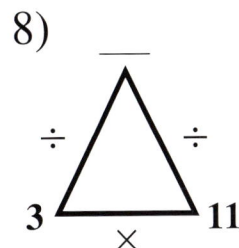

9)
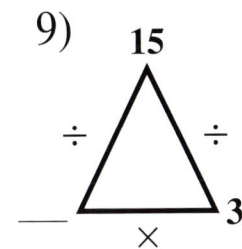

10)
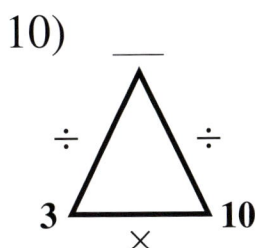

Score

ae © 2016 Stephen Curran

6. Division by 4

Division means to share out something equally.

For example:

There are **20** items. If these are shared out between **4** children, they will each have **5** items.

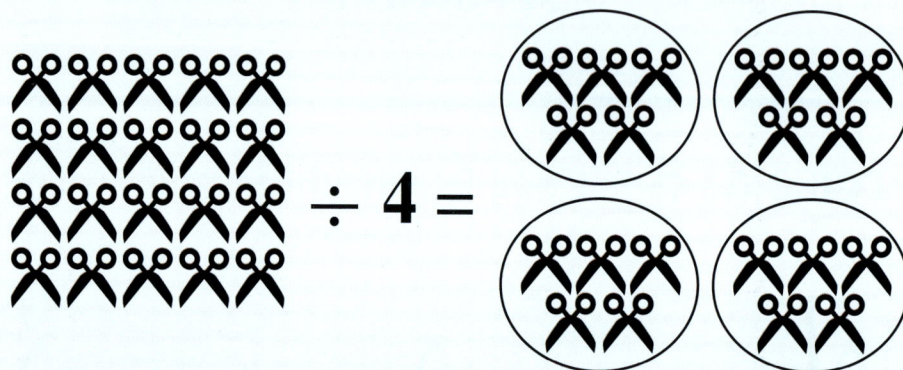

$$\div 4 =$$

This can be written as:

$$20 \div 4 = 5$$

Example: Calculate **8 ÷ 4**.

When dividing by **4**, the number is being shared or split into **four** groups.

8 shared out between **four** groups means there are **2** in each group.

Answer: **8 ÷ 4 = 2**

Exercise 5: 6   Calculate the following:

1) **16 ÷ 4** = _____

2) $0 \div 4 =$ _____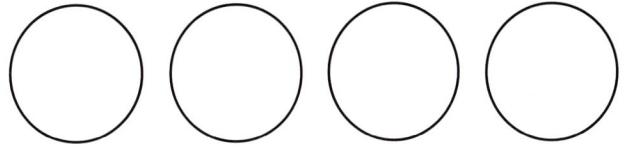

3) $48 \div 4 =$ _____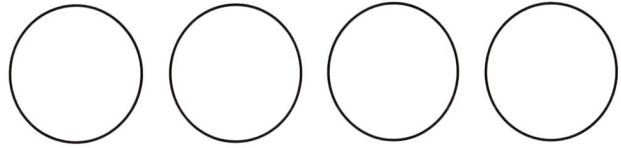

4) $32 \div 4 =$ _____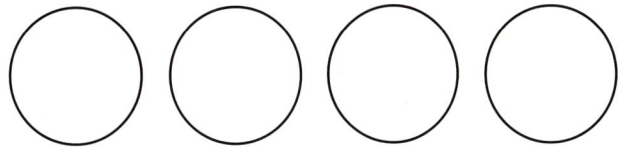

5) $24 \div 4 =$ _____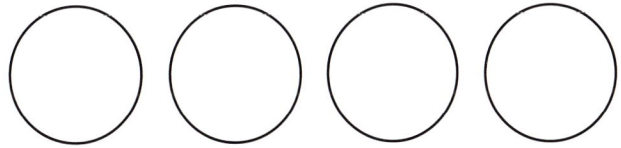

6) $40 \div 4 =$ _____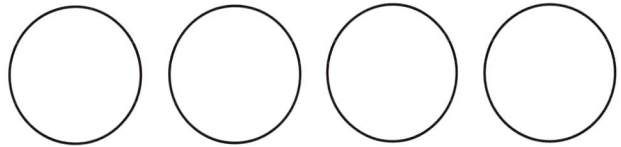

7) $12 \div 4 =$ _____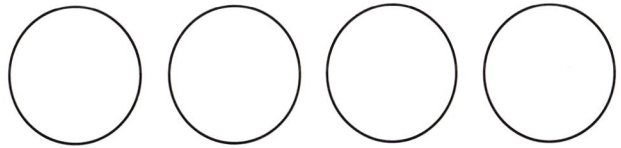

8) $36 \div 4 =$ _____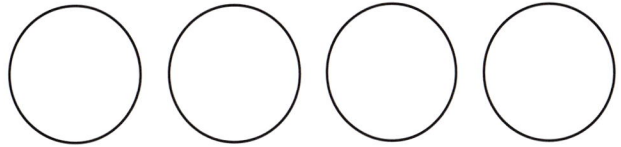

9) $4 \div 4 =$ _____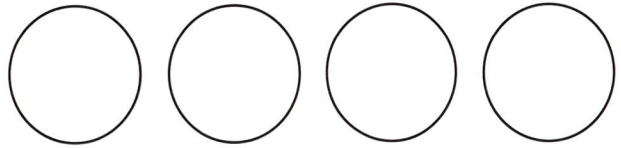

10) $28 \div 4 =$ _____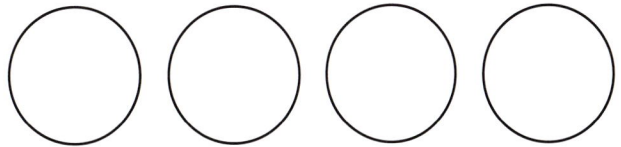

Score

Example: Complete the times table triangle.

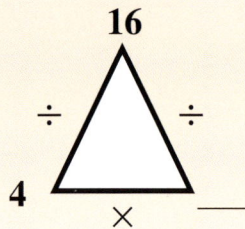

Divide the top number by the number on the left-hand side of the triangle.

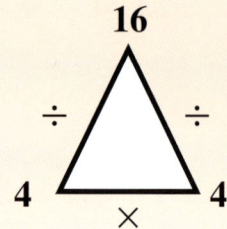

16 ÷ 4 = 4

Exercise 5: 7   Complete the times tables triangle:

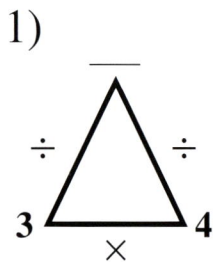

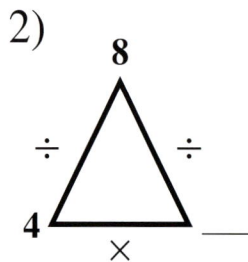

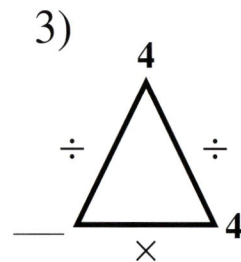

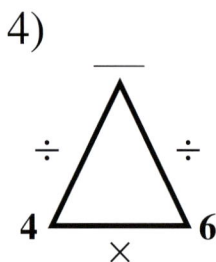

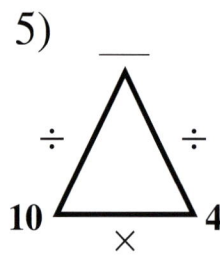

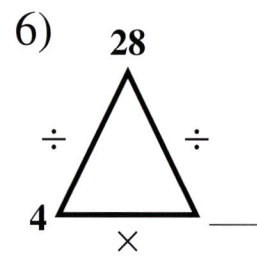

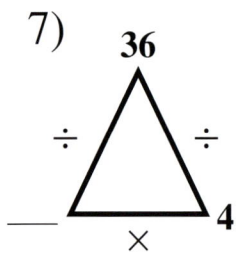

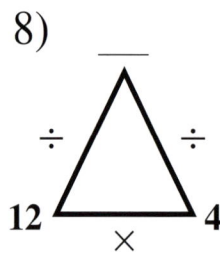

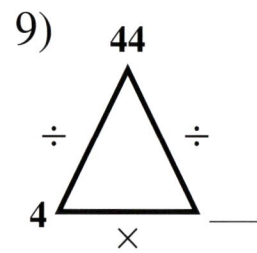

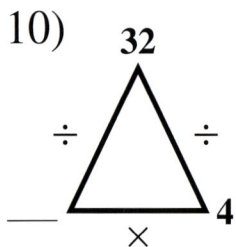

1)

2)

3)

4)

5)

6)

7)

8)

9)

10)

Score

7. Division by 5

Division means to share out something equally.

For example:

There are **30** items. If these are shared out between **5** children, they will each have **6** items.

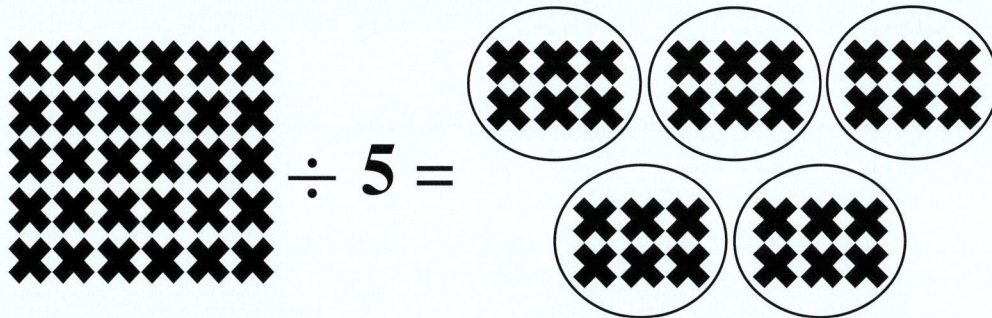

This can be written as:

$$30 \div 5 = 6$$

Example: Calculate **5 ÷ 5**.

When dividing by **5**, the number is being shared or split into **five** groups.

5 shared out between **five** groups means there is **1** in each group.

Answer: **5 ÷ 5 = 1**

Exercise 5: 8   Calculate the following:

Score

1) **25 ÷ 5 = _____**   2) **45 ÷ 5 = _____**

3) $35 \div 5 =$ _____   4) $15 \div 5 =$ _____

5) $50 \div 5 =$ _____   6) $20 \div 5 =$ _____

7) $10 \div 5 =$ _____   8) $60 \div 5 =$ _____

9) $40 \div 5 =$ _____   10) $55 \div 5 =$ _____

Example: | Complete the times table triangle.

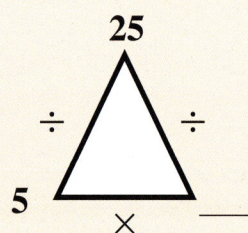

Divide the top number by the number on the left-hand side of the triangle.

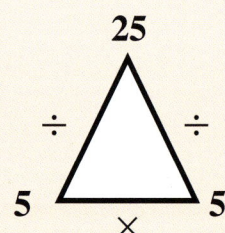

$$25 \div 5 = 5$$

Exercise 5: 9   Complete the times tables triangle:

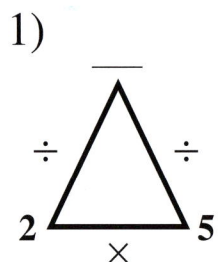

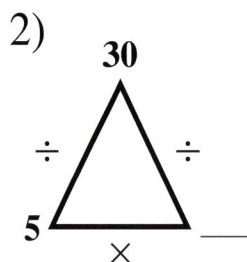

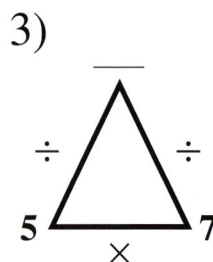

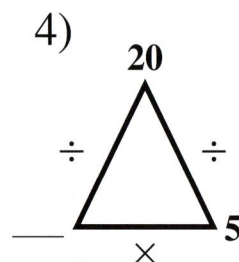

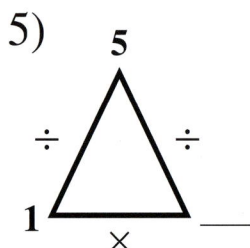

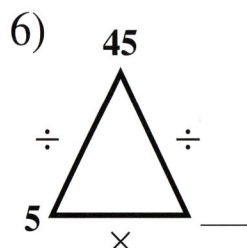

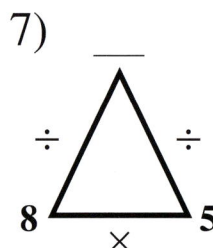

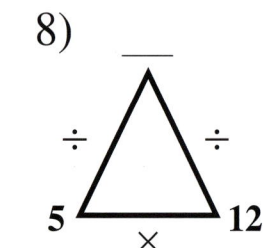

1)   2) top 30   3)   4) top 20

5) top 5   6) top 45   7)   8)

9) 55
$\div$ △ $\div$
___   5
    $\times$

10) 15
$\div$ △ $\div$
5   ___
    $\times$

Score

8. Division by 6

Division means to share out something equally.

For example:

There are **42** items. If these are shared out between **6** children, they will each have **7** items.

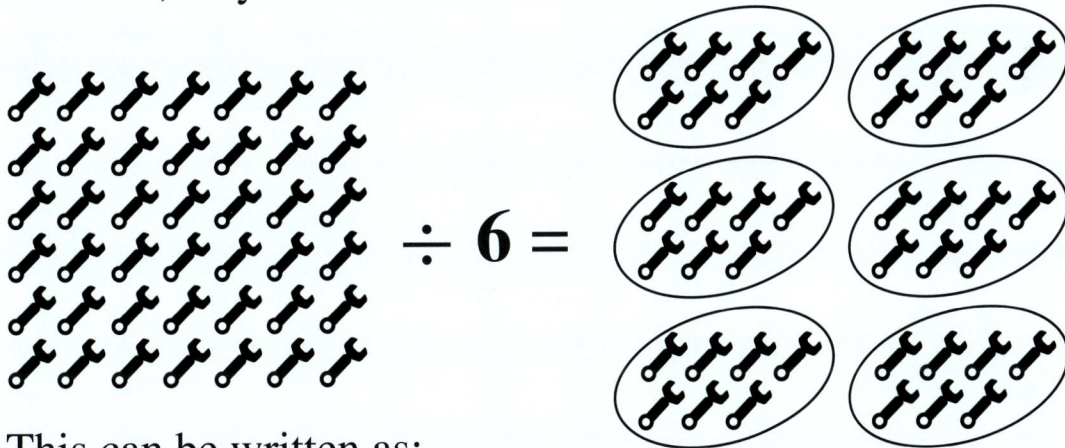

$\div\ 6 =$

This can be written as:

$$42 \div 6 = 7$$

Example: Calculate **54 ÷ 6**.

When dividing by **6**, the number is being shared or split into **six** groups.

54 shared out between **six** groups means there are **9** in each group.

9 9 9 9 9 9

Answer: **54 ÷ 6 = 9**

Exercise 5: 10 Calculate the following:

1) $12 \div 6 =$ _____

2) $0 \div 6 =$ _____

3) $24 \div 6 =$ _____

4) $36 \div 6 =$ _____

5) $48 \div 6 =$ _____

6) $72 \div 6 =$ _____

7) $30 \div 6 =$ _____

8) $6 \div 6 =$ _____

9) $66 \div 6 =$ _____

10) $18 \div 6 =$ _____

Example: | Complete the times table triangle.

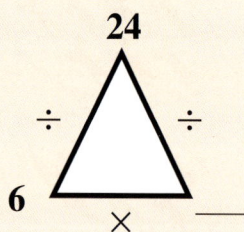

Divide the top number by the number on the left-hand side of the triangle.

$$24 \div 6 = 4$$

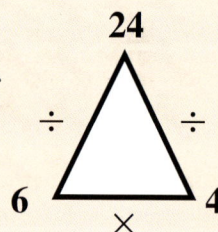

Exercise 5: 11 Complete the times tables triangle:

1)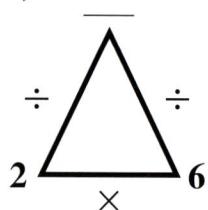

2)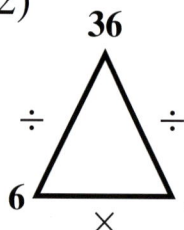

3)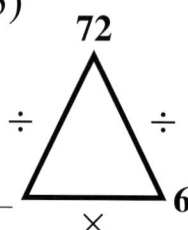

4)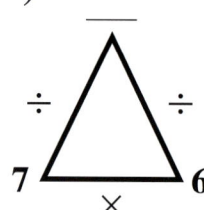

5)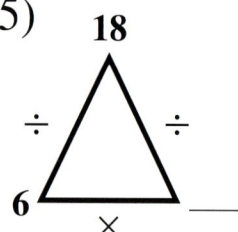

6)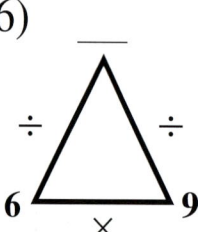

7)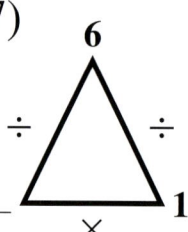

8)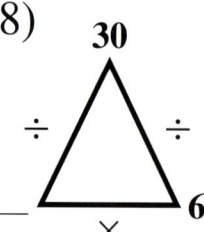

9) $\underline{\quad}$

÷ △ ÷

10 ⟍△⟋ 6
  ×

10) $\underline{\quad}$

÷ △ ÷

6 ⟍△⟋ 8
  ×

Score

9. Division by 7

Division means to share out something equally.

For example:

There are **56** items. If these are shared out between **7** children, they will each have **8** items.

 ÷ 7 =

This can be written as:

$$56 \div 7 = 8$$

Example: Calculate **28 ÷ 7**.

When dividing by **7**, the number is being shared or split into **seven** groups.

28 shared out between **seven** groups means there are **4** in each group.

④ ④ ④ ④ ④ ④ ④

Answer: **28 ÷ 7 = 4**

Exercise 5: 12 Calculate the following:

1) $49 \div 7 =$ _____

2) $7 \div 7 =$ _____

3) $63 \div 7 =$ _____

4) $21 \div 7 =$ _____

5) $77 \div 7 =$ _____

6) $35 \div 7 =$ _____

7) $14 \div 7 =$ _____

8) $42 \div 7 =$ _____

9) $0 \div 7 =$ _____

10) $84 \div 7 =$ _____

Example: | Complete the times table triangle.

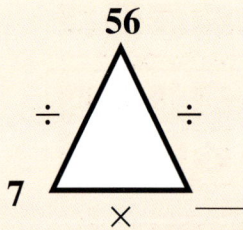

Divide the top number by the number on the left-hand side of the triangle.

$$56 \div 7 = 8$$

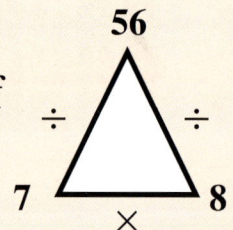

Exercise 5: 13 Complete the times tables triangle:

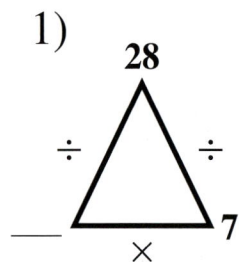

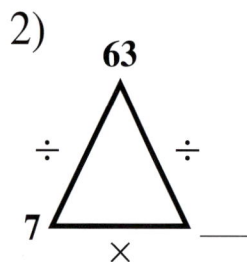

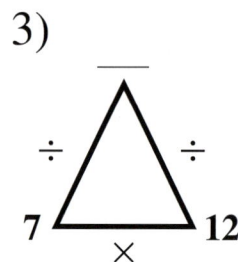

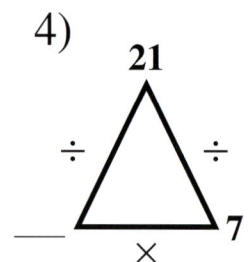

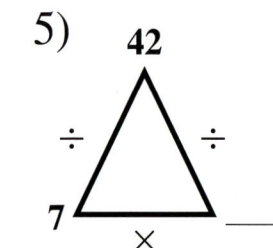

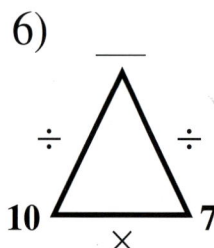

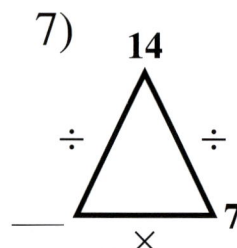

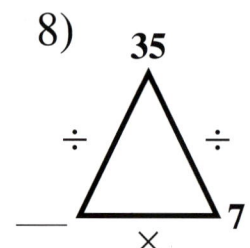

1) 28

7

2) 63

7

3) ___

7   12

4) 21

7

5) 42

7

6) ___

10   7

7) 14

7

8) 35

7

10. Division by 8

Division means to share out something equally.

For example:

There are **72** items. If these are shared out between **8** children, they will each have **9** items.

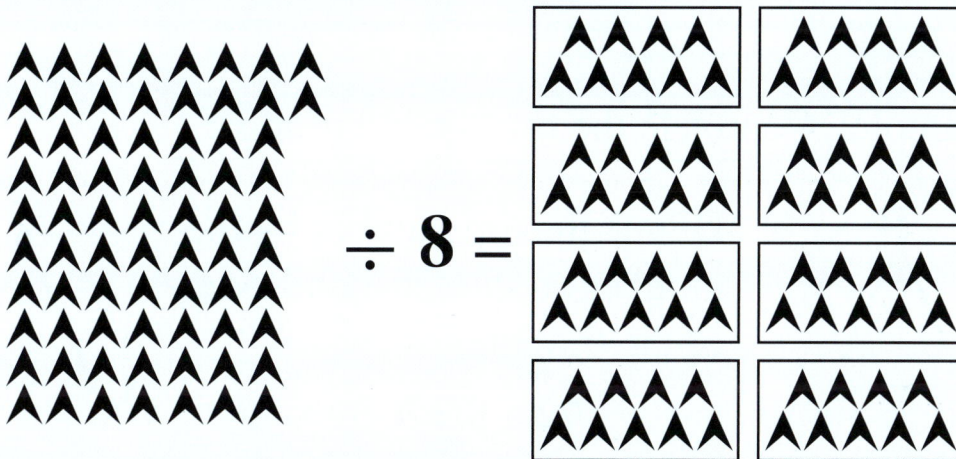

$$\div\ 8\ =$$

This can be written as:

$$72 \div 8 = 9$$

Example: Calculate $24 \div 8$.

When dividing by **8**, the number is being shared or split into **eight** groups.

24 shared out between **eight** groups means there are **3** in each group.

3 3 3 3 3 3 3 3

Answer: $24 \div 8 = 3$

Exercise 5: 14　Calculate the following:

1) $48 \div 8 = $ _____

2) $40 \div 8 = $ _____

3) $16 \div 8 = $ _____

4) $80 \div 8 = $ _____

5) $0 \div 8 = $ _____

6) $56 \div 8 = $ _____

7) $96 \div 8 = $ _____

8) $32 \div 8 = $ _____

9) $64 \div 8 = $ _____

10) $88 \div 8 = $ _____

Example: | Complete the times table triangle. |

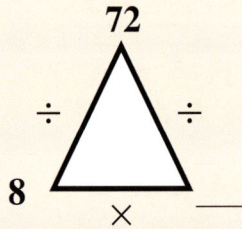

Divide the top number by the number on the left-hand side of the triangle.

$$72 \div 8 = 9$$

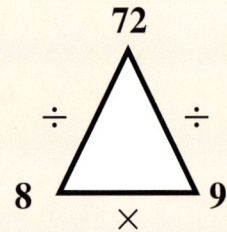

Exercise 5: 15　Complete the times tables triangle:

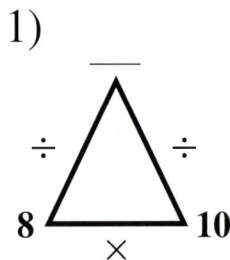

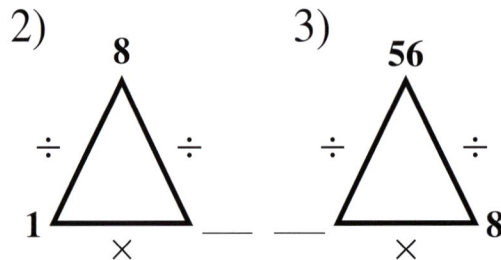

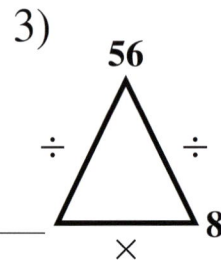

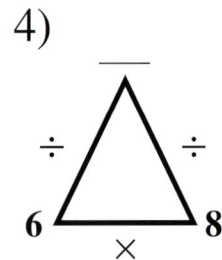

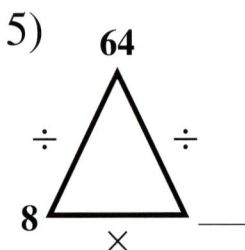

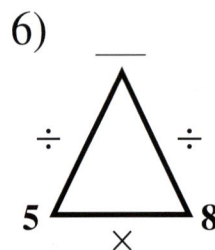

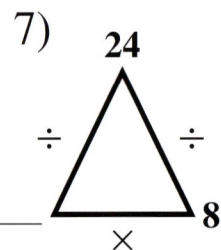

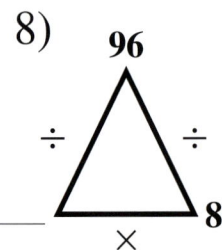

1) 2) 3) 4)

5) 6) 7) 8)

9)

$$32$$
$$\div \quad \div$$
$$8 \qquad \underline{\quad}$$
$$\times$$

10)

$$\underline{\quad}$$
$$\div \quad \div$$
$$2 \qquad 8$$
$$\times$$

11. Division by 9

Division means to share out something equally.

For example:

There are **81** items. If these are shared out between **9** children, they will each have **9** items.

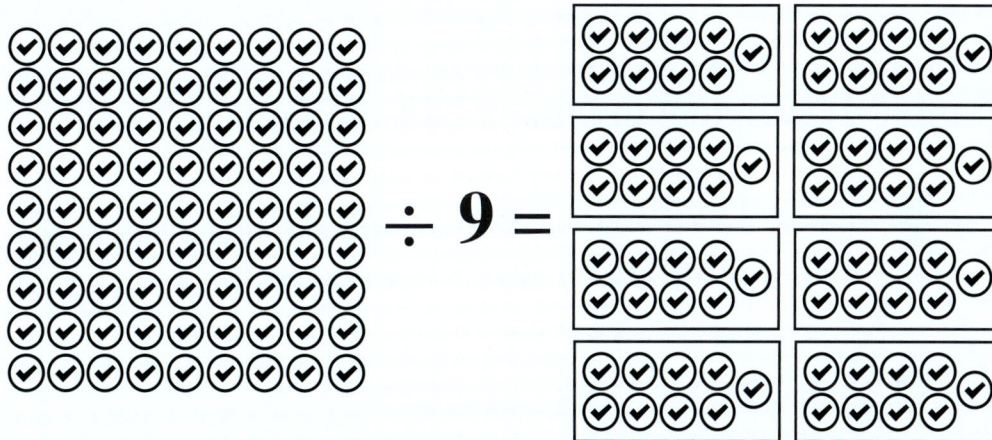

This can be written as:

$$81 \div 9 = 9$$

Example: Calculate **99 ÷ 9**.

When dividing by **9**, the number is being shared or split into **nine** groups.

99 shared out between **nine** groups means there are **11** in each group.

Answer: **99 ÷ 9 = 11**

Exercise 5: 16 Calculate the following:

1) $72 \div 9 =$ _____

2) $45 \div 9 =$ _____

3) $36 \div 9 =$ _____

4) $54 \div 9 =$ _____

5) $18 \div 9 =$ _____

6) $63 \div 9 =$ _____

7) $108 \div 9 =$ _____

8) $9 \div 9 =$ _____

9) $27 \div 9 =$ _____

10) $90 \div 9 =$ _____

Example: | Complete the times table triangle. |

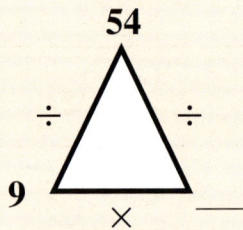

Divide the top number by the number on the left-hand side of the triangle.

$$54 \div 9 = 6$$

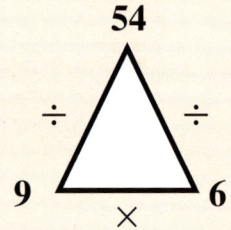

Exercise 5: 17 Complete the times tables triangle:

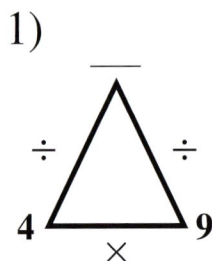

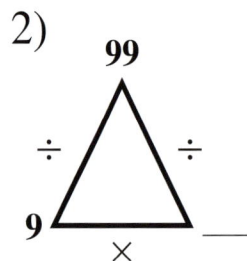

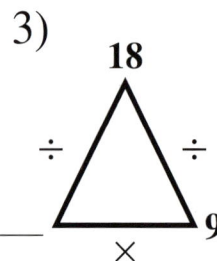

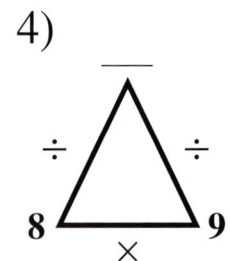

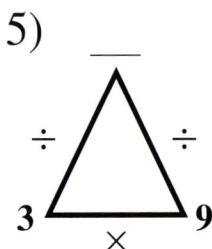

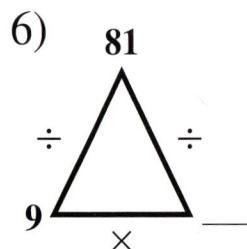

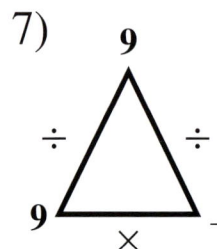

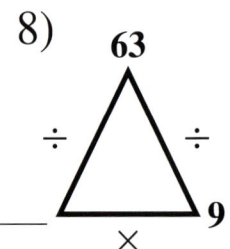

1)

2) 99

3) 18

4)

5)

6) 81

7) 9

8) 63

9)

$\div$ $\triangle$ $\div$
45
___ 9
$\times$

10)

$\div$ $\triangle$ $\div$
___
12 9
$\times$

Score

12. Division by 10

Division means to share out something equally.

For example:

There are **70** items. If these are shared out between **10** children, they will each have **7** items.

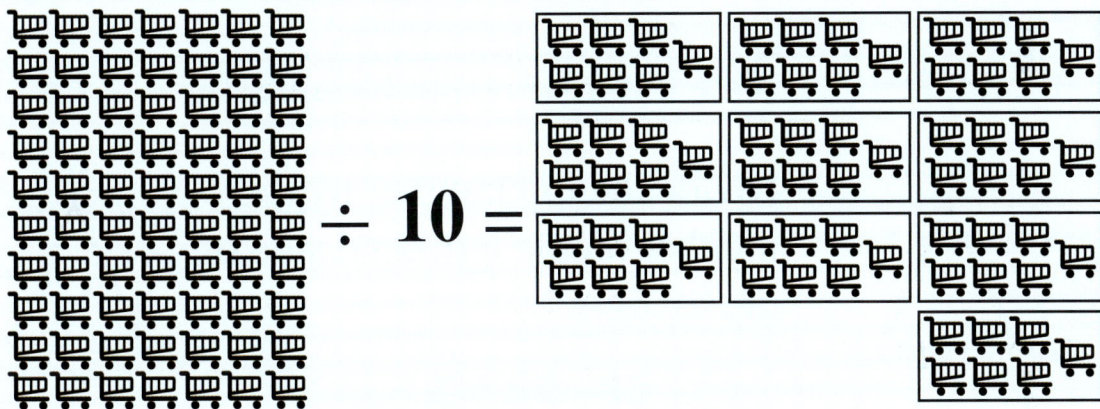

$\div$ **10** =

This can be written as:

$$70 \div 10 = 7$$

Example: | Calculate **90 $\div$ 10**. |

When dividing by **10**, the number is being shared or split into **ten** groups.

90 shared out between **ten** groups means there are **9** in each group.

9 9 9 9 9 9 9 9 9 9

Answer: **90 $\div$ 10 = 9**

Exercise 5: 18 Calculate the following:

1) $10 \div 10 =$ _____

2) $40 \div 10 =$ _____

3) $100 \div 10 =$ _____

4) $80 \div 10 =$ _____

5) $60 \div 10 =$ _____

6) $20 \div 10 =$ _____

7) $50 \div 10 =$ _____

8) $110 \div 10 =$ _____

9) $120 \div 10 =$ _____

10) $30 \div 10 =$ _____

Example: | Complete the times table triangle. |

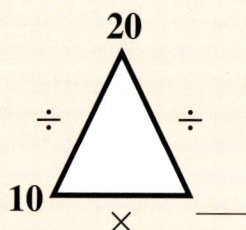

Divide the top number by the number on the left-hand side of the triangle.

$$20 \div 10 = 2$$

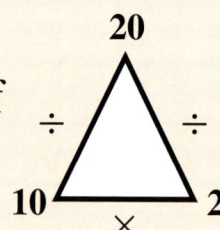

Exercise 5: 19 Complete the times tables triangle:

1) 9 ÷ × 10 (top: ___)

2) 10 ÷ × ___ (left: 10, top: 10)

3) 40 ÷ × ___ (left: 10)

4) 120 ÷ × ___ (left: 10)

5) 30 ÷ × 10 (left: ___)

6) 60 ÷ × ___ (left: 10)

7) ___ ÷ × 10 (left: 11)

8) ___ ÷ × 10 (left: 8)

9)

$\div$ △ $\div$

10 × 10

10) 50

$\div$ △ $\div$

___ × 5

Score

a. Division by Tens

Dividing by multiples of **10** is very easy to do.

To divide by **10**, remove one **zero** (**0**) from the end.

$20 \div 10 = 2$

T	U
2	0

$\div 10 \longrightarrow$

U
2

To divide by **100**, remove two **zeros** (**00**) from the end.

$200 \div 100 = 2$

H	T	U
2	0	0

$\div 100 \longrightarrow$

U
2

To divide by **1,000**, remove three **zeros** (**000**) from the end.

$2,000 \div 1,000 = 2$

Th	H	T	U
2	0	0	0

$\div 1,000 \longrightarrow$

U
2

Example: | Calculate **3,000 ÷ 100**. |

Count the number of zeros on the dividing number (**100**) and remove the same number of zeros from the number being divided into. **3,000** with two zeros removed will become **3,0̶0̶0̶**.

$$3,000 \div 100 = 30$$

Answer: **30**

Score

Exercise 5: 20   Calculate the following:

1) $40 \div 10 =$ _____

2) $720 \div 10 =$ _____

3) $390 \div 10 =$ _____

4) $5,100 \div 100 =$ _____

5) $6,300 \div 100 =$ _____

6) $12,800 \div 100 =$ _____

7) $58{,}000 \div 1{,}000 = $ _____   8) $93{,}000 \div 1{,}000 = $ _____

9) $80{,}000 \div 1{,}000 = $ _____   10) $27{,}000 \div 1{,}000 = $ _____

13. Division by 11

Division means to share out something equally.

For example:

There are **22** items. If these are shared out between **11** children, they will each have **2** items.

This can be written as:

$$22 \div 11 = 2$$

Example: Calculate **88 ÷ 11**.

When dividing by **11**, the number is being shared or split into **eleven** groups.

88 shared out between **eleven** groups means there are **8** in each group.

Answer: $88 \div 11 = 8$

Exercise 5: 21 Calculate the following:

1) $121 \div 11 = $ _____

2) $0 \div 11 = $ _____

3) $77 \div 11 = $ _____

4) $44 \div 11 = $ _____

5) $99 \div 11 = $ _____

6) $132 \div 11 = $ _____

7) $110 \div 11 = $ _____

8) $33 \div 11 = $ _____

9) $66 \div 11 = $ _____

10) $55 \div 11 = $ _____

Example: | Complete the times table triangle.

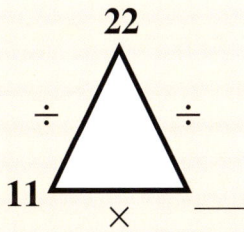

Divide the top number by the number on the left-hand side of the triangle.

$$22 \div 11 = 2$$

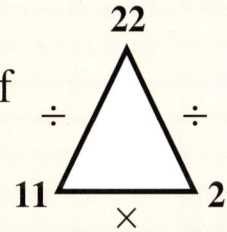

Exercise 5: 22 Complete the times tables triangle:

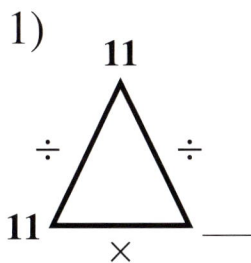

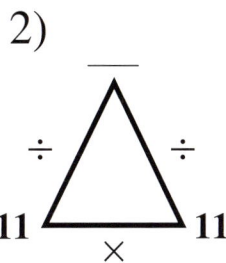

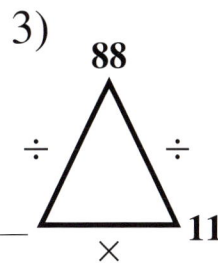

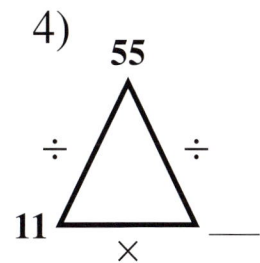

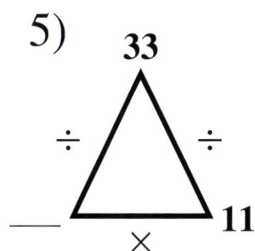

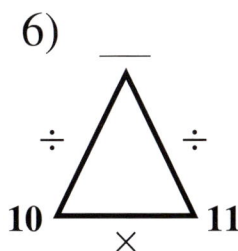

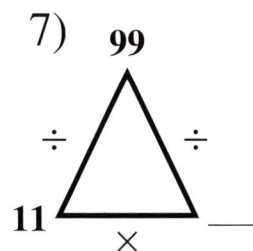

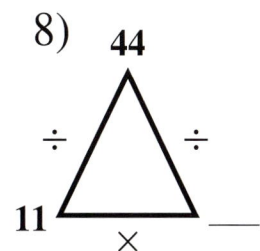

1)

2)

3)

4)

5)

6)

7)

8)

9)

$$77$$
$$\div \triangle \div$$
$$\underline{\quad} \qquad 11$$
$$\times$$

10)

$$\underline{\quad}$$
$$\div \triangle \div$$
$$11 \qquad 12$$
$$\times$$

14. Division by 12

Division means to share out something equally.

For example:

There are **48** items. If these are shared out between **12** children, they will each have **4** items.

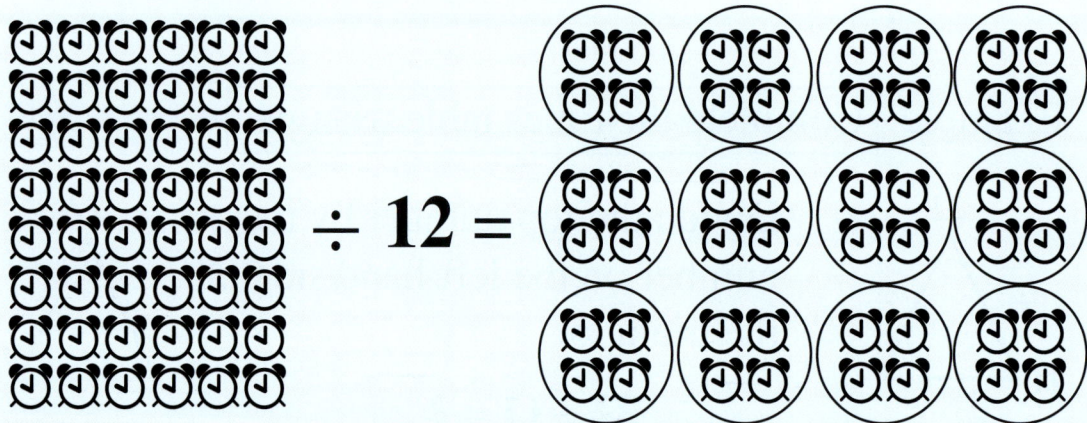

$$\div \; 12 \; =$$

This can be written as:

$$48 \div 12 = 4$$

Example: Calculate **120 ÷ 12.**

When dividing by **12**, the number is being shared or split into **twelve** groups.

120 shared out between **twelve** groups means there are **10** in each group.

(10) (10) (10) (10) (10) (10) (10) (10) (10) (10)
(10) (10)

Answer: **120 ÷ 12 = 10**

Exercise 5: 23 Calculate the following:

1) $84 \div 12 =$ _____

2) $12 \div 12 =$ _____

3) $72 \div 12 =$ _____

4) $96 \div 12 =$ _____

5) $36 \div 12 =$ _____

6) $108 \div 12 =$ _____

7) $144 \div 12 =$ _____

8) $60 \div 12 =$ _____

9) $24 \div 12 =$ _____

10) $132 \div 12 =$ _____

Example: | Complete the times table triangle. |

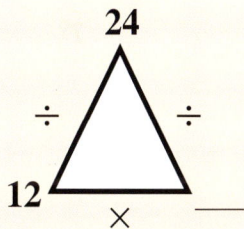

24

Divide the top number by the number on the left-hand side of the triangle.

$24 \div 12 = 2$

24

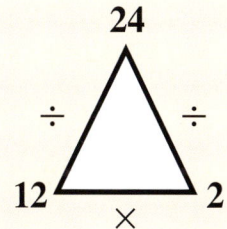

Exercise 5: 24 Complete the times tables triangle:

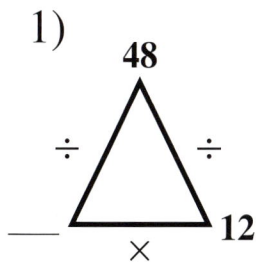

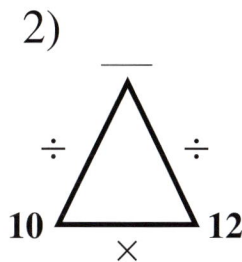

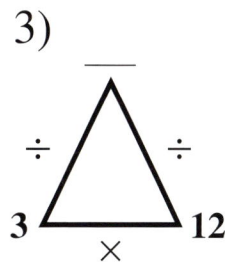

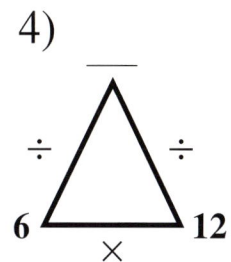

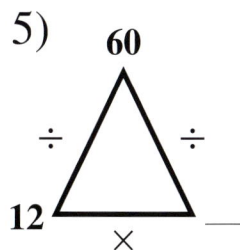

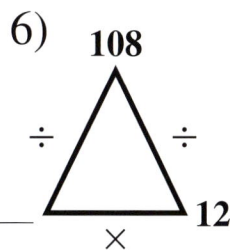

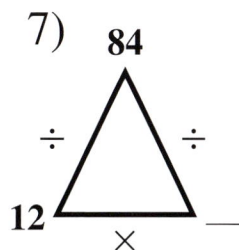

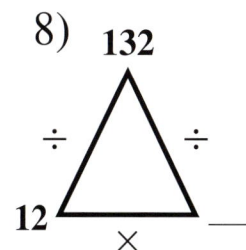

1) 48 ÷ __ △ ÷ 12 ×

2) __ ÷ 10 △ ÷ 12 ×

3) __ ÷ 3 △ ÷ 12 ×

4) __ ÷ 6 △ ÷ 12 ×

5) 60 ÷ 12 △ ÷ __ ×

6) 108 ÷ __ △ ÷ 12 ×

7) 84 ÷ 12 △ ÷ __ ×

8) 132 ÷ 12 △ ÷ __ ×

9) $\dfrac{}{\underset{12 \quad \times \quad 12}{\div \triangle \div}}$

10) $\dfrac{12}{\underset{12 \quad \times \quad }{\div \triangle \div}}$

Score

15. Number Sentences

Exercise 5: 25 Calculate the following:

Score

1) $84 \div 12 =$ _____

2) $36 \div 6 =$ _____

3) $18 \div 9 =$ _____

4) $21 \div 7 =$ _____

5) $50 \div 5 =$ _____

6) $64 \div 8 =$ _____

7) $42 \div 7 =$ _____

8) $16 \div 4 =$ _____

9) $56 \div 8 =$ _____

10) $108 \div 12 =$ _____

Exercise 5: 26 Fill in the missing spaces:

Score

1) _____ $\div 9 = 12$

2) $100 \div 10 =$ _____

3) $20 \div$ _____ $= 4$

4) $18 \div$ _____ $= 3$

5) $132 \div 11 =$ _____

6) _____ $\div 8 = 9$

7) _____ $\div 4 = 6$

8) $56 \div 7 =$ _____

9) $24 \div$ _____ $= 2$

10) _____ $\div 3 = 7$

16. Short Division

If a number does not divide exactly there will be something left over. This is called a **remainder**.

For example:

If there are **7** marbles in a bag to be shared between **3** children, each child will receive **2** marbles and there will be **1** marble left over.

Left over marble or remainder.

$$7 \div 3 = 2 \text{ rem. } 1$$

The following terminology applies to all division calculations:

Quotient → 2 rem. 1 ← Remainder

Dividing Number → $3\overline{)7}$ ← Number Divided Into

- The number being divided into is placed to the right of the division bracket.

- The dividing number is placed outside the division bracket.

- The answer is called the **quotient** and is written above the bracket.

- The left over is the **remainder** and is also written above the bracket.

a. Standard Short Division

Standard Short Division involves dividing each digit individually, carrying the tens and units and writing the answers above the line.

(i) Without Remainders

Example: | Calculate **462 ÷ 2**.

2 divides into **4** twice, to give the answer **2**.
2 divides into **6** three times, to give the answer **3**.
2 divides into **2** once, to give the answer **1**.

Answer: **231**

$$\begin{array}{c} 2\ 3\ 1 \\ \hline 2\,|\,4\ 6\ 2 \end{array}$$

Exercise 5: 27a   Calculate the following:

1) $3\,|\,6\ 3\ 9$ 2) $2\,|\,8\ 2\ 0$ 3) $5\,|\,5\ 0\ 5$

Example: | Calculate **148 ÷ 4**.

Step 1 - Divide the hundreds.

1 ÷ 4 cannot be divided, so write **0** in the answer and carry the left over **1** hundred.

$$\begin{array}{c} 0 \\ \hline 4\,|\,1\ {}^1 4\ 8 \end{array}$$

Step 2 - Divide the tens.

14 ÷ 4 = 3 remainder **2**

Write **3** in the answer because
3 × 4 = 12

The remainder is **2** because
14 − 12 = 2

$$\begin{array}{c} 0\ 3 \\ \hline 4\,|\,1\ {}^1 4\ {}^2 8 \end{array}$$

Carry remainder **2** into the units column.

Step 3 - Divide the units.

$28 \div 4 = 7$ remainder **0**

Write **7** in the answer because

$7 \times 4 = 28$

There is nothing left over.

$$4\overline{)1\,4^1\,2\,8}\;\;037$$

Answer: **37**

Exercise 5: 27b   Calculate the following:

4) $4\overline{)848}$ 5) $9\overline{)126}$ 6) $7\overline{)287}$

7) $936 \div 6$ 8) $315 \div 3$

9) $492 \div 4$ 10) $728 \div 8$

(ii) With Remainders

Example: Calculate **907 ÷ 5**.

Step 1 - Divide the hundreds.

$9 \div 5 = 1$ remainder **4**

Write **1** in the answer.

The remainder is calculated by mental subtraction ($9 - 5 = 4$).

Carry remainder **4** into the tens column.

$$5\overline{)9^4\,0\,7}\;\;1$$

Step 2 - Divide the tens.

$40 \div 5 = 8$ remainder 0

Write **8** in the answer because
$8 \times 5 = 40$

$$5 \overline{)9^4 0\ 7}^{1\ 8}$$

Step 3 - Divide the units.

$7 \div 5 = 1$ remainder 2

Write **1** in the answer because
$1 \times 5 = 7$
The remainder is **2** because
$7 - 5 = 2$

$$5 \overline{)9^4 0\ 7}^{1\ 8\ 1\ \text{rem. } 2}$$

There are **2** units left over.

Answer: **181 rem. 2**

Exercise 5: 28   Calculate the following:

1) $4 \overline{)8\ 4\ 5}$ rem. _____

2) $3 \overline{)3\ 6\ 5}$ rem. _____

3) $5 \overline{)5\ 5\ 6}$ rem. _____

4) $2 \overline{)4\ 6\ 9}$ rem. _____

5) $6 \overline{)1\ 3\ 5}$ rem. _____

6) $9 \overline{)9\ 7\ 8}$ rem. _____

7) **267 ÷ 7**   8) **652 ÷ 5**

⌐¯¯¯¯¯¯¯ **rem.**   ⌐¯¯¯¯¯¯¯ **rem.**

9) **697 ÷ 3**   10) **739 ÷ 8**

⌐¯¯¯¯¯¯¯ **rem.**   ⌐¯¯¯¯¯¯¯ **rem.**

Score

b. Partitioning

Partitioning means to break up numbers into smaller parts, making calculations easier.

For example, **24** can be partitioned into **20** and **4** (**2** tens and **4** units).

Example: | Calculate **49 ÷ 8**. |

                                        TU
Step 1 - Split the first number: **49 = 40** and **9**

Step 2 - Divide the tens: **40 ÷ 8 = 5**

Step 3 - Divide the units: **9 ÷ 8 = 1 rem. 1**

Step 4 - Add the answers together: **5 + 1 rem. 1 = 6 rem. 1**

Answer: **6 rem. 1**

Exercise 5: 29   Calculate the following:

1) **39 ÷ 6**

   39 = [_30_ & _9_]

   _30_ ÷ _6_ = _5_

   _9_ ÷ _6_ = _1 rem. 3_

   _5_ + _1 rem. 3_ = _____

2) **79 ÷ 9**

   79 = [_70_ & _9_]

   _70_ ÷ _9_ = _7 rem. 7_

   _9_ ÷ _9_ = _1_

   7 rem. 7 + _1_ = _____

3) **78 ÷ 7**

   78 = [_70_ & _8_]

   _70_ ÷ _7_ = _____

   _8_ ÷ _7_ = _____

   _____ + _____ = _____

4) **86 ÷ 5**

   86 = [_80_ & _6_]

   _80_ ÷ _5_ = _____

   _6_ ÷ _5_ = _____

   _____ + _____ = _____

5) **95 ÷ 3**

   95 = [_____ & _____]

   ___ ÷ _3_ = _____

   ___ ÷ _3_ = _____

   _____ + _____ = _____

6) **46 ÷ 8**

   46 = [_____ & _____]

   ___ ÷ _8_ = _____

   ___ ÷ _8_ = _____

   _____ + _____ = _____

7) **137 ÷ 5**

   137 = [_100_ & _37_]

   ___ ÷ ___ = _____

   ___ ÷ ___ = _____

   _____ + _____ = _____

8) **113 ÷ 2**

   113 = [_____ & _____]

   ___ ÷ ___ = _____

   ___ ÷ ___ = _____

   _____ + _____ = _____

9) **235 ÷ 4**

235 = [_200_ & _35_]

___ ÷ ___ = _____

___ ÷ ___ = _____

_____ + _____ = _____

10) **258 ÷ 8**

258 = [____ & ____]

___ ÷ ___ = _____

___ ÷ ___ = _____

_____ + _____ = _____

c. Expanded Short Division

Expanded Short Division involves repeated subtraction of the dividing number from the number being divided.

The dividing number can be grouped into larger chunks and repeatedly subtracted to find the answer and any remainders.

It is sometimes called 'chunking'.

Example: Calculate **110 ÷ 6**.

This is set out in a similar way to standard short division.

Step 1 - Group the divisor into the largest simple chunk; **10** groups of **6**.

$6 \times 10 = 60$

Subtract from **110**.

$110 - 60 = 50$

```
        rem.
6 ) 1 1 0
      6 0   (6 × 10)
      5 0
```

Step 2 - The next largest amount that can be subtracted is **8** groups of **6**.

$6 \times 8 = 48$

Then subtract from **50**.

$50 - 48 = 2$

This is the remainder, as **2** cannot be made into another group of **6**, as it is too small.

$$
\begin{array}{r}
\text{rem. 2} \\
6\,\overline{)\,1\,1\,0} \\
6\,0 \quad (6 \times 10) \\
\overline{5\,0} \\
4\,8 \quad (6 \times 8) \\
\overline{2}
\end{array}
$$

Step 3 - Add up the number of **6s** that have been subtracted to find the answer.

$10 + 8 = 18$

The last subtraction gave the remainder of **2**.

$$
\begin{array}{r}
1\,8 \quad \text{rem. 2} \\
6\,\overline{)\,1\,1\,0} \\
6\,0 \quad 6 \times \boxed{10} \\
\overline{5\,0} \\
4\,8 \quad 6 \times \boxed{8}\,+ \\
\overline{2} \quad \boxed{18}
\end{array}
$$

Answer: **18 rem. 2**

Score

Exercise 5: 30   Calculate the following:

1)

$$
\begin{array}{r}
8\,\overline{)\,9\,6} \\
8\,0 \quad (8 \times 10) \\
\overline{1\,6} \\
1\,6 \quad (8 \times 2)\,+ \\
\overline{0}
\end{array}
$$

2)

$$
\begin{array}{r}
5\,\overline{)\,8\,5} \\
5\,0 \quad (5 \times 10) \\
\overline{3\,5} \\
3\,5 \quad (5 \times 7)\,+ \\
\overline{0}
\end{array}
$$

3)

$$6\overline{)90}$$

___ (6 × 10)

___ (6 × 5) +

4)

$$4\overline{)76}$$

___ (4 × 10)

___ (4 × 9) +

5)

$$3\overline{)54}$$

___ (×)

___ (×) +

6)

$$7\overline{)91}$$

___ (×)

___ (×) +

7) **rem.**

$$6\overline{)76}$$

6 0 (6 × 10)

1 6

1 2 (6 × 2) +

4

8) **rem.**

$$8\overline{)94}$$

___ (×)

___ (×) +

9) **rem.**

$$7\overline{)115}$$

___ (×)

___ (×) +

10) **rem.**

$$9\overline{)131}$$

___ (×)

___ (×) +

17. Division in Words

There are many different terms for division.

Here is a list of the most commonly used terms:

- Share
- Divide
- Find the quotient
- Partition
- Separate or split into equal groups

- Halve (divide by **2**)
- Find a third (divide by **3**)
- Quarter (divide by **4**)

Example: | Share out **one hundred and thirty-seven** among **seven**.

Convert the words into a number sentence. 'Share' is the same thing as using the ÷ sign between the numbers.

The number sentence is **137 ÷ 7**.

It is best to solve this using standard short division.

$$7 \overline{)1\,3\,^67} = 1\,9 \text{ rem. } 4$$

Answer: **19 rem. 4**

Exercise 5: 31   Answer the following:

Score

1) Share **one hundred and thirty-two** between **eleven**. ____

2) Halve **one hundred and fifty-two**. _____

3) How many **eights** are there in **six hundred and seventy-eight**? _____

4) Quarter **eight hundred and ninety-six**. _____

5) What is the quotient of **four hundred and three** divided by **seven**? _____

6) Divide **two hundred and thirty-four** by **nine**. _____

7) Group **four hundred and ninety-eight** into **fives**. _____

8) How many **threes** are there in **seven hundred and sixteen**? _____

9) Divide **three hundred and fifty-six** by **six**. _____

10) Group **one hundred and forty-four** into **twelves**. _____

18. Inverse Operations

It is useful to understand the relationship between multiplication and division. **Inverse means Opposite.**

$\times$ and $\div$ are a pair of inverse operations.
The inverse of multiplication is division.

$$8 \times 12 = 96$$
$$96 \div 8 = 12$$
$$96 \div 12 = 8$$

For every multiplication calculation there are two division calculations that relate to it as inverse operations. This can be represented using a triangle.

Example: Show the three calculations that link **44**, **8** and **352**.

There are one multiplication and two division calculations that demonstrate how these numbers relate to each other.

Multiplication	1st Division	2nd Division
44×8	$352 \div 44$	$352 \div 8$

$$\begin{array}{r} 4\,4 \\ 8 \times \\ \hline 3\,5\,2 \end{array}$$

$$44\overline{)\,3\,5\,2\,}\;\;^{8}$$

$$8\overline{)\,3\,5\,2\,}\;\;^{4\,4}$$

Answer: $44 \times 8 = 352$

$352 \div 44 = 8$

$352 \div 8 = 44$

Exercise 5: 32   Calculate the following:

Score

1-2)

$$11\overline{)\,6\,6\,}\;\;^{\boxed{6}}$$

$$\begin{array}{r} 1\,1 \\ 6 \times \\ \hline \boxed{} \end{array}$$

$$6\overline{)\,6\,6\,}\;\;^{\boxed{}}$$

3-4)

$$12\overline{)\,8\,4\,}\;\;^{\boxed{7}}$$

$$\begin{array}{r} \boxed{} \\ 7 \times \\ \hline 8\,4 \end{array}$$

$$7\overline{)\,\boxed{}\,}\;\;^{1\,2}$$

5-7)

$$\begin{array}{r} 9\,1 \\ 2 \times \\ \hline \boxed{} \end{array}$$

$$\boxed{}\overline{)\,1\,8\,2\,}\;\;^{9\,1}$$

$$\boxed{}\overline{)\,1\,8\,2\,}\;\;^{2}$$

8-10)

$$66 \times \boxed{} = 264$$

$$4 \overline{\smash{\big)}\,264} = \boxed{}$$

$$66 \overline{\smash{\big)}\,\boxed{}} = 4$$

19. Problem Solving

Example: There are **43** passengers waiting to go to the airport. If each taxi seats **4** people, how many taxis are needed?

Step 1 - Divide the total number of passengers by the number of seats in each taxi.

$$4 \overline{\smash{\big)}\,43} = 10 \text{ rem. } 3$$

Convert the problem into a number sentence:

$$43 \div 4 = 10 \text{ rem. } 3$$

Step 2 - As there is a remainder of **3**, there are **3** people left without a taxi, meaning an extra taxi is needed.

$$10 + 1 = 11$$

Answer: **11 taxis**

Exercise 5: 33   Answer the following:

Score

1) Alaina has **seventy-six** Christmas cards. She gives them out to **two** equal size classes of children and has **twelve** left. How many children are in each class? ____

2) If Steve has **twenty-six** shoes, how many pairs of shoes does he have? ____

3) Sanjana and Huzaefa are playing a game. If they get the same score and their total score is **374**, what score did they each get? ____

4) **Nine** children take part in a reading challenge. **74** books are read altogether. If **one** child reads **10** books and the rest read the same amount of books, how many books does each of these children read? ____

5) A delivery of **108** items is delivered in **9** boxes. How many items are in each box? ____

6) A school trip of **75** students and **5** teachers are going to the theatre. If each row has **8** seats, how many rows will they fill? ____

7) A zoo is assigning keepers to animals. If there are **96** animals and **8** keepers, how many animals are assigned to each keeper? ____

8) Cakes are sold in packs of **six**. How many packs will contain **seven hundred and twenty-six** cakes? ____

9) A child has **seven** packs of **42** cards. In a game with **six** children, how many cards does each child get? ____

10) A box of **72** highlighters is divided between **2** classes. If each child is given **2** highlighters, how many children are there in each class? ____

Answers

Chapter Four
Multiplication

Exercise 4: 1a
1) 0   2) 0
3) 0   4) 0
5) 0

Exercise 4: 1b
6) 5   7) 9
8) 4   9) 6
10) 7

Exercise 4: 2
1) 3   2) 4
3) 5   4) 6
5) 7   6) 1
7) 9   8) 1
9) 11   10) 12

Exercise 4: 3a
1) 6   2) 12
3) 14   4) 8
5) 16

Exercise 4: 3b
6) 12   7) 18
8) 8   9) 14
10) 6

Exercise 4: 4
1) 3   2) 8
3) 5   4) 12
5) 14   6) 2
7) 9   8) 2
9) 22   10) 24

Exercise 4: 5a
1) 6   2) 15
3) 18   4) 9
5) 24

Exercise 4: 5b
6) 12   7) 18
8) 9   9) 21
10) 27

Exercise 4: 6
1) 9   2) 4
3) 15   4) 6
5) 3   6) 24
7) 3   8) 10
9) 33   10) 3

Exercise 4: 7a
1) 20   2) 24
3) 28   4) 16
5) 36

Exercise 4: 7b
6) 28   7) 12
8) 36   9) 32
10) 20

Exercise 4: 8
1) 4   2) 4
3) 20   4) 24
5) 7   6) 4
7) 36   8) 10
9) 4   10) 48

Exercise 4: 9a
1) 10   2) 20
3) 35   4) 30
5) 40

Exercise 4: 9b
6) 35   7) 10
8) 45   9) 30
10) 15

Exercise 4: 10
1) 3   2) 5
3) 25   4) 6
5) 35   6) 5
7) 45   8) 10
9) 5   10) 60

Exercise 4: 11a
1) 30   2) 24
3) 36   4) 48
5) 42

Exercise 4: 11b
6) 48   7) 12
8) 54   9) 30
10) 42

Exercise 4: 12
1) 3   2) 24
3) 30   4) 6
5) 7   6) 48
7) 54   8) 6
9) 11   10) 72

Exercise 4: 13
1) 21   2) 28
3) 35   4) 42
5) 49   6) 56
7) 63   8) 70
9) 77   10) 84

Exercise 4: 14
1) 7   2) 14
3) 77   4) 42
5) 7   6) 5
7) 63   8) 49
9) 8   10) 84

Exercise 4: 15
1) 24   2) 32
3) 40   4) 48
5) 56   6) 64
7) 72   8) 80
9) 88   10) 96

Exercise 4: 16
1) 32   2) 8
3) 2   4) 56
5) 40   6) 8
7) 8   8) 80
9) 96   10) 72

Exercise 4: 17
1) 27   2) 36
3) 45   4) 54
5) 63   6) 72

7) 81   8) 90
9) 99   10) 108

Exercise 4: 18
1) 9   2) 90
3) 9   4) 36
5) 1   6) 9
7) 63   8) 5
9) 9   10) 12

Exercise 4: 19a
1) 50   2) 70
3) 60   4) 40
5) 80

Exercise 4: 19b
6) 20   7) 70
8) 50   9) 80
10) 90

Exercise 4: 20
1) 3   2) 40
3) 50   4) 10
5) 7   6) 80
7) 9   8) 100
9) 10   10) 120

Exercise 4: 21
1) 40
2) 190
3) 1,840
4) 6,200
5) 9,900
6) 20,700
7) 3,000
8) 51,000
9) 739,000
10) 485,000

Exercise 4: 22
1) 33   2) 44
3) 55   4) 66
5) 77   6) 88
7) 99   8) 110
9) 121 10) 132

Answers

Exercise 4: 23
1) 11   2) 77
3) 11   4) 6
5) 2   6) 10
7) 88   8) 11
9) 132   10) 121

Exercise 4: 24
1) 36   2) 48
3) 60   4) 72
5) 84   6) 96
7) 108   8) 120
9) 132   10) 144

Exercise 4: 25
1) 24   2) 4
3) 84   4) 60
5) 8   6) 12
7) 108   8) 132
9) 12   10) 144

Exercise 4: 26

×	2	3	4	5	6	7	8	9	10	11	12
2	4	6	8	10	12	14	16	18	20	22	24
1) **3**	6	9	12	15	18	21	24	27	30	33	36
2) **4**	8	12	16	20	24	28	32	36	40	44	48
3) **5**	10	15	20	25	30	35	40	45	50	55	60
4) **6**	12	18	24	30	36	42	48	54	60	66	72
5) **7**	14	21	28	35	42	49	56	63	70	77	84
6) **8**	16	24	32	40	48	56	64	72	80	88	96
7) **9**	18	27	36	45	54	63	72	81	90	99	108
8) **10**	20	30	40	50	60	70	80	90	100	110	120
9) **11**	22	33	44	55	66	77	88	99	110	121	132
10) **12**	24	36	48	60	72	84	96	108	120	132	144

Exercise 4: 27

×	3	8	11	6	4	9	12	2	10	7	5
2	6	16	22	12	8	18	24	4	20	14	10
1) **7**	21	56	77	42	28	63	84	14	70	49	35
2) **4**	12	32	44	24	16	36	48	8	40	28	20
3) **10**	30	80	110	60	40	90	120	20	100	70	50
4) **6**	18	48	66	36	24	54	72	12	60	42	30
5) **3**	9	24	33	18	12	27	36	6	30	21	15
6) **9**	27	72	99	54	36	81	108	18	90	63	45
7) **11**	33	88	121	66	44	99	132	22	110	77	55
8) **5**	15	40	55	30	20	45	60	10	50	35	25
9) **12**	36	96	132	72	48	108	144	24	120	84	60
10) **8**	24	64	88	48	32	72	96	16	80	56	40

Exercise 4: 28
1) 35   2) 48
3) 0   4) 108
5) 56   6) 24
7) 27   8) 28
9) 12   10) 55

Exercise 4: 29
1) 96   2) 0
3) 7   4) 42
5) 4   6) 44
7) 10   8) 12
9) 7   10) 6

Exercise 4: 30
1) $16 = [10 \& 6]$
$10 \times 3 = 30$
$6 \times 3 = 18$
$30 + 18 = 48$
2) $13 = [10 \& 3]$
$10 \times 9 = 90$
$3 \times 9 = 27$
$90 + 27 = 117$
3) $18 = [10 \& 8]$
$10 \times 4 = 40$
$8 \times 4 = 32$
$40 + 32 = 72$
4) $13 = [10 \& 3]$
$10 \times 5 = 50$
$3 \times 5 = 15$
$50 + 15 = 65$
5) $18 = [10 \& 8]$
$10 \times 6 = 60$
$8 \times 6 = 48$
$60 + 48 = 108$
6) $15 = [10 \& 5]$
$10 \times 9 = 90$
$5 \times 9 = 45$
$90 + 45 = 135$
7) $14 = [10 \& 4]$
$10 \times 7 = 70$
$4 \times 7 = 28$
$70 + 28 = 98$
8) $19 = [10 \& 9]$
$10 \times 2 = 20$
$9 \times 2 = 18$
$20 + 18 = 38$
9) $14 = [10 \& 4]$
$10 \times 8 = 80$
$4 \times 8 = 32$
$80 + 32 = 112$
10) $16 = [10 \& 6]$
$10 \times 7 = 70$
$6 \times 7 = 42$
$70 + 42 = 112$

Exercise 4: 31
1) 1,782   2) 2,295
3) 3,367   4) 532
5) 4,664   6) 1,392
7) 1,935   8) 7,245
9) 6,741   10) 2,472

Exercise 4: 32
1) 36   2) 18
3) 36   4) 14
5) 21   6) 24
7) 32   8) 30
9) 54   10) 35

Exercise 4: 33
1) 679   2) 72
3) 290   4) 592
5) 57   6) 207
7) 180   8) 408
9) 738   10) 392

Exercise 4: 34
1) 1,647   2) 1,872
3) 7,456   4) 924
5) 1,278   6) 1,516
7) 4,046   8) 2,379
9) 4,075   10) 5,934

Exercise 4: 35
1) 2,387   2) 4,968

Answers

3) 2,877   4) 1,068
5) 1,580   6) 4,055
7) 1,264   8) 5,984
9) 3,978   10) 1,422

Exercise 4: 36
1) 124   2) 126
3) 25   4) 8
5) 546   6) 38
7) 36   8) 192
9) 144   10) 868

Chapter Five
Division
Exercise 5: 1
1) 5   2) 2
3) 1   4) 9
5) 7   6) 1
7) 3 – 1 – 1 – 1 = 0
8) 2 – 1 – 1 = 0
9) 1 ÷ 1 = 1
10) 4 ÷ 1 = 4

Exercise 5: 2
1) 3   2) 8
3) 2   4) 6
5) 10   6) 1
7) 9   8) 11
9) 7   10) 12

Exercise 5: 3
1) 24   2) 6
3) 16   4) 7
5) 3   6) 2
7) 20   8) 2
9) 5   10) 8

Exercise 5: 4
1) 8   2) 0
3) 9   4) 3
5) 12   6) 2
7) 6   8) 10
9) 1   10) 7

Exercise 5: 5
1) 4   2) 6
3) 6   4) 21
5) 12   6) 3
7) 3   8) 33
9) 5   10) 30

Exercise 5: 6
1) 4   2) 0
3) 12   4) 8
5) 6   6) 10
7) 3   8) 9
9) 1   10) 7

Exercise 5: 7
1) 12   2) 2
3) 1   4) 24
5) 40   6) 7
7) 9   8) 48
9) 11   10) 8

Exercise 5: 8
1) 5   2) 9
3) 7   4) 3
5) 10   6) 4
7) 2   8) 12
9) 8   10) 11

Exercise 5: 9
1) 10   2) 6
3) 35   4) 4
5) 5   6) 9
7) 40   8) 60
9) 11   10) 3

Exercise 5: 10
1) 2   2) 0
3) 4   4) 6
5) 8   6) 12
7) 5   8) 1
9) 11   10) 3

Exercise 5: 11
1) 12   2) 6

3) 12   4) 42
5) 3   6) 54
7) 6   8) 5
9) 60   10) 48

Exercise 5: 12
1) 7   2) 1
3) 9   4) 3
5) 11   6) 5
7) 2   8) 6
9) 0   10) 12

Exercise 5: 13
1) 4   2) 9
3) 84   4) 3
5) 6   6) 70
7) 2   8) 5
9) 7   10) 1

Exercise 5: 14
1) 6   2) 5
3) 2   4) 10
5) 0   6) 7
7) 12   8) 4
9) 8   10) 11

Exercise 5: 15
1) 80   2) 8
3) 7   4) 48
5) 8   6) 40
7) 3   8) 12
9) 4   10) 16

Exercise 5: 16
1) 8   2) 5
3) 4   4) 6
5) 2   6) 7
7) 12   8) 1
9) 3   10) 10

Exercise 5: 17
1) 36   2) 11
3) 2   4) 72
5) 27   6) 9

7) 1   8) 7
9) 5   10) 108

Exercise 5: 18
1) 1   2) 4
3) 10   4) 8
5) 6   6) 2
7) 5   8) 11
9) 12   10) 3

Exercise 5: 19
1) 90   2) 1
3) 4   4) 12
5) 3   6) 6
7) 110   8) 80
9) 100   10) 10

Exercise 5: 20
1) 4   2) 72
3) 39   4) 51
5) 63   6) 128
7) 58   8) 93
9) 80   10) 27

Exercise 5: 21
1) 11   2) 0
3) 7   4) 4
5) 9   6) 12
7) 10   8) 3
9) 6   10) 5

Exercise 5: 22
1) 1   2) 121
3) 8   4) 5
5) 3   6) 110
7) 9   8) 4
9) 7   10) 132

Exercise 5: 23
1) 7   2) 1
3) 6   4) 8
5) 3   6) 9
7) 12   8) 5
9) 2   10) 11

Answers

Exercise 5: 24
1) 4   2) 120
3) 36   4) 72
5) 5   6) 9
7) 7   8) 11
9) 144   10) 1

Exercise 5: 25
1) 7   2) 6
3) 2   4) 3
5) 10   6) 8
7) 6   8) 4
9) 7   10) 9

Exercise 5: 26
1) 108   2) 10
3) 5   4) 6
5) 12   6) 72
7) 24   8) 8
9) 12   10) 21

Exercise 5: 27a
1) 213   2) 410
3) 101

Exercise 5: 27b
4) 212   5) 14
6) 41   7) 156
8) 105   9) 123
10) 91

Exercise 5: 28
1) 211 rem. 1
2) 121 rem. 2
3) 111 rem. 1
4) 234 rem. 1
5) 22 rem. 3
6) 108 rem. 6
7) 38 rem. 1
8) 130 rem. 2
9) 232 rem. 1
10) 92 rem. 3

Exercise 5: 29
1) 39 = [30 & 9]
   $30 \div 6 = 5$
   $9 \div 6 = 1$ rem. 3
   5 + 1 rem. 3 = 6 rem. 3
2) 79 = [70 & 9]
   $70 \div 9 = 7$ rem. 7
   $9 \div 9 = 1$
   7 rem. 7 + 1 = 8 rem. 7
3) 78 = [70 & 8]
   $70 \div 7 = 10$
   $8 \div 7 = 1$ rem. 1
   10 + 1 rem. 1 = 11 rem. 1
4) 86 = [80 & 6]
   $80 \div 5 = 16$
   $6 \div 5 = 1$ rem. 1
   16 + 1 rem. 1 = 17 rem. 1
5) 95 = [90 & 5]
   $90 \div 3 = 30$
   $5 \div 3 = 1$ rem. 2
   30 + 1 rem. 2 = 31 rem. 2
6) 46 = [40 & 6]
   $40 \div 8 = 5$
   $6 \div 8 = 0$ rem. 6
   5 + 0 rem. 6 = 5 rem. 6
7) 137 = [100 & 37]
   $100 \div 5 = 20$
   $37 \div 5 = 7$ rem. 2
   20 + 7 rem. 2 = 27 rem. 2
8) 113 = [100 & 13]
   $100 \div 2 = 50$
   $13 \div 2 = 6$ rem. 1
   50 + 6 rem. 1 = 56 rem. 1
9) 235 = [200 & 35]
   $200 \div 4 = 50$
   $35 \div 4 = 8$ rem. 3
   50 + 8 rem. 3 = 58 rem. 3
10) 258 = [200 & 58]
   $200 \div 8 = 25$
   $58 \div 8 = 7$ rem. 2
   25 + 7 rem. 2 = 32 rem. 2

Exercise 5: 30
1) 12
2) 17
3) 15
4) 19
5) 18
6) 13
7) 12 rem. 4
8) 11 rem. 6
9) 16 rem. 3
10) 14 rem. 5

Exercise 5: 31
1) 12
2) 76
3) 84 rem. 6
4) 224
5) 57 rem. 4
6) 26
7) 99 rem. 3
8) 238 rem. 2
9) 59 rem. 2
10) 12

Exercise 5: 32
1) 66   2) 11
3) 12   4) 84
5) 182   6) 2
7) 91   8) 4
9) 66   10) 264

Exercise 5: 33
1) 32   2) 13
3) 187   4) 8
5) 12   6) 10
7) 12   8) 121
9) 49   10) 18

PROGRESS CHARTS

Shade in your score for each exercise on the graph. Add up for your total score.

4. MULTIPLICATION

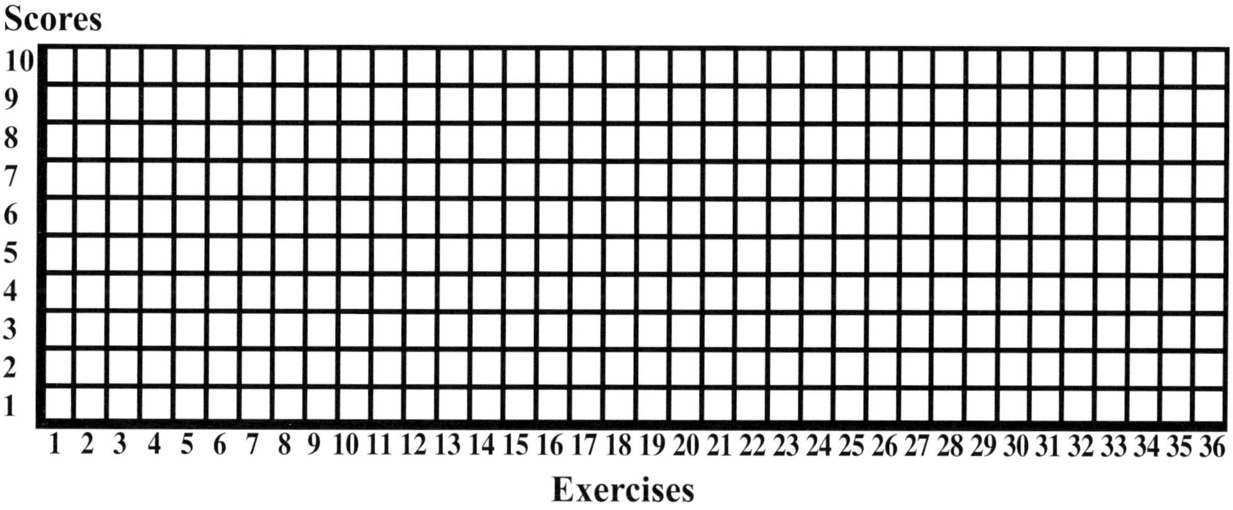

Scores

Graph with scores 1-10 on the y-axis and exercises 1-36 on the x-axis	Total Score
	Percentage
	%

1 2 3 4 5 6 7 8 9 10 11 12 13 14 15 16 17 18 19 20 21 22 23 24 25 26 27 28 29 30 31 32 33 34 35 36

Exercises

5. DIVISION

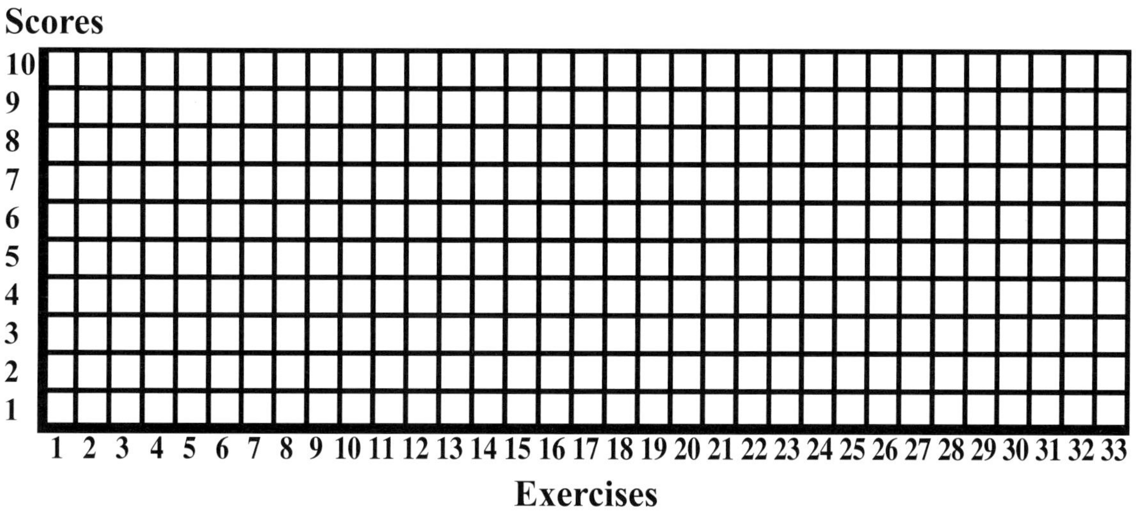

Scores

Graph with scores 1-10 on the y-axis and exercises 1-33 on the x-axis	Total Score
	Percentage
	%

1 2 3 4 5 6 7 8 9 10 11 12 13 14 15 16 17 18 19 20 21 22 23 24 25 26 27 28 29 30 31 32 33

Exercises

Overall Percentage %

CERTIFICATE OF

ACHIEVEMENT

This certifies

_____

has successfully completed

Key Stage 2 Maths
Year 3/4
WORKBOOK **3**

Overall percentage
score achieved

☐ **%**

Comment _____

_____

Signed _____

(teacher/parent/guardian)

Date _____